Diet Lifestyle

Lose Weight with Comfort Foods and Grain Free Recipes

Christy Burgess and Camille Edwards

Table of Contents

Introduction

Do you realize that dieting is a lifestyle? You cannot look at going on a "diet" as a temporary thing. Failure often occurs with diets when people go on a diet long enough to lose the weight (or lower blood pressure or lower cholesterol) and then go right back to the old eating habits. You need to stop and consider why you are in the health predicament you are in - it is because of your old eating habits. If you have gained weight, you gained it because of your eating habits and probably lack of exercise.

When you need to diet to change your physical health, you need to make the diet a lifestyle change. This means you will forget about your old eating habits and will take on new, healthier eating habits. But before you can make a successful lifestyle change you need to break the bad eating habits you may have first. If you don't break these bad habits you run the risk of going through "food withdrawal" symptoms.

Food withdrawal symptoms might include headaches, intense cravings, and moodiness. This is especially true if the food addiction is for sugar. Sugar is one of the most intense addictions and going "cold turkey" may cause some intense cravings for it. Instead of suffering through the withdrawal symptoms, you should slowly wean from the junk food before diving into the new diet plan. You can start the new diet while weaning. Taking the time to wean first will help you to get on and stick with the new diet.

It takes the body about three weeks to break a bad habit. You can break most any habit by doing a slow wean over three weeks, including weaning from alcohol, cigarettes, and even recreational drugs. Of course, you should never try to wean from those on your own and you should seek the guidance of your health care provider. But weaning from food is safer. Here are a couple of ways to wean from junk food successfully. Just remember even if you cheat do not be hard on yourself. Just pick back up where you were and keep going with it.

If you want to give it a week to start, just eat as you normally do and keep a food journal. Record what you eat and how much you eat. If you really want to dive into your eating habits, you should also record how you are feeling. See if you notice any patterns such as stress eating, or happy eating, or bored eating. Ideally, you should only eat when hungry but so many people do not and will eat during other times. This is a great contributor to the obesity factor.

One way to wean is to count how many times a day you eat junk food. You will want to start eliminating ONE time a day for about three days in a row before eliminating another time. Repeat every three days by adding another instance of replacing the junk food with something more nutritious like fruit, nuts, or leftovers (if you are cooking the recipes from this book). By three weeks, you will have safely weaned from the junk food and the withdrawals symptoms should be at minimum if any at all.

Another way to wean from the junk food is to assess how much you eat. If you eat a lot of junk food during the day, say three or more times start with limiting to eating it just three times a day for about five days. Then move down to two times a day for five days. Then move down to once a day for five days. Then move to every other day. Then put two days between eating it. And follow up until you are only eating it once a week. By that point, you may be able to let it go completely. At first, view the eating of junk food as a reward for sticking with the diet.

The hope is that your body will stop craving the junk food. It takes time, which is why the weaning process works so well. By the time you have weaned you may no longer crave junk food. You will be eating healthy.

Exercise

When you make a dieting lifestyle change, you should also include exercise. The body thrives with physical activity. Adding exercise helps to increase the metabolism, which gives you more energy to continue with physical activity. Physical activity also helps the body to release endorphins, which are a "feel good" substance. This is a way to achieve a "natural high," squash depression, and lift the mood without the harmful side effects of prescription medications.

In order to exercise properly you only need to commit to doing it every other day at minimum. A good workout is normally achieved within a half an hour. You can start with something as easy as a five-minute warm up of stretches followed by a vigorous walk of twenty minutes and ending with a five-minute cool down stretch. You can also ride a bike; do aerobics, swim, and workout at a gym. The idea is to do enough vigorous exercise that the body burns the calories and releases the endorphins. You may have heard of the "runner's high," which is achieved by runners when they run for a certain amount of time. You don't have to run to achieve this; any good physical exercise if done for long enough, will bring on the release of the endorphins.

Disclaimer

As with anything you do for your health, always seek the guidance of your health care provider. If you have any existing health concerns, you need to clear any diet or exercise through them. Take all the advice given here as informational purposes only. The diets are healthy and most physicians will agree they are okay. Exercise is always beneficial; however, make sure it will be for you as well. You will get out of this diet what you put into it.

Section 1: Grain Free Recipes

There's something absolutely delicious about a freshly baked loaf of bread, a crispy waffle, or a tasty cake hot out of the oven! These foods all have one thing in common: they're made with grain or wheat flour. Cooking with wheat flour and grain is something that everyone does, and it produces a whole lot of delicious foods.

Unfortunately for many, grain and wheat are things that they cannot enjoy. Gluten intolerance can be a serious problem for many people, and they are unable to eat foods that contain lots of grain or wheat. When they do, they have serious digestive problems, or their body can react strongly and negatively to the gluten in the grain that they are eating.

Gluten has been linked to a number of problems. Interestingly enough, the body often sees gluten as being a foreign substance that it can't process. While gluten is commonly found in the food we eat, it wasn't always part of our diet. The human body can't always process this gooey, sticky protein easily, and it can be a bit hard on the body if you happen to be sensitive to it. Even those without celiac problems may not be able to handle the gluten, as their bodies react to the "foreign substance" by attacking it with antibodies.

Cutting grain out of your diet can help to reduce your risk of health problems, especially if you have celiac disorder or other gluten-sensitive problems. However, even for those that don't have these health problems, it may be a good idea to cut gluten out of your diet. Many people don't have celiac disease, and yet they still experience the drawbacks of eating gluten.

In an article in the New Zealand edition of Stuff magazine, an article by a world-renowned expert on food allergies, Dr. Rodney Ford, states, "Gluten causes tiredness, anxiety and stress. The medical world accepts it can damage the gut, but it can also damage the brain, skin and nerves. Until now, many of these illnesses have been blamed on everything from stress at home to other medical conditions, including depression." [1]

Cutting gluten out of your life isn't just something you can do to prevent celiac problems, but it can be good for your health. Many holistic doctors and therapists will recommend cutting it from your diet, as it carries the risk of causing negative side effects.

Did you know that eliminating grain and gluten can be beneficial to your body? The benefits include:

- Reduced risk of IBS or other digestive problems
- Less chance of becoming fatigued, depressed, nauseous, or developing stomach cramps
- Boost in your energy levels
- Reduced body fat percentage
- Increase in lean muscle tissue
- Lowered blood pressure
- Improved mood and sense of wellbeing
- As you can see, there are many great reasons to cut grain from your diet!

"But," you may say, "all of my favorite foods are made with grain! How can I cut grain out of my diet and still enjoy the food I'm eating?"

Don't worry about it! In this book, you'll find plenty of delicious recipes that you can make without needing to use grain, and you can whip up your favorite dishes and still make them gluten-free. You'll have to spend a bit of money to stock your house with some ingredients you probably don't have right now, but you'll be amazed at how many delicious foods you can make without using grain.

Enjoy the book, and happy grain-free cooking!

Tasty Grain Free Recipes

Grain Free Breaded Chicken

There's nothing like some breaded chicken to kick off your lunch in style, but bread crumbs have wheat, right? Here is a quick and easy recipe you can use to make breaded chicken without the bread...

Ingredients

For this dish, you will need:

1 large chicken breast
1 cup of almond flour
½ cup of Kraft's Parmesan Cheese
Thyme
Basil
Oregano
½ cup of butter
Red or crushed chili pepper
Garlic powder
Salt and pepper, to taste

Preparation:

To begin, slice the chicken breast into steaks -- preferably about three steaks from each half of the breast. You should have about 6 medium steaks from the breast.

Preheat your oven to about 350 F. Use a bit of butter to grease the bottom of a baking tray.

In a bowl, combine the almond flour with the Parmesan cheese. Sprinkle in about a teaspoon each of basil, thyme, and oregano, and add in a pinch of crushed red pepper for some spice. A teaspoon of garlic powder will help to add the flavor you want, and a bit of salt and black pepper will round out the flavors.

In a saucepan, melt the butter. Dip the chicken steaks into the butter, ensuring that the entire surface of the chicken is coated well. Roll the buttered strips in the almond flour, and make sure that they are properly coated with the flour mixture.

Place the steaks onto your baking tray, laying them as flat as possible. Transfer the tray into the oven, and let the steaks cook for about 20 minutes. They should be a wonderful golden brown, and they will be absolutely delightful to eat! (Check to make sure that they aren't pink in the center, as that's a sign that the chicken is undercooked.)

Sesame Seed Chicken Fried Steak

Want to eat that Southern-style chicken fried steak that your mama used to make you? This simple recipe won't make it exactly like the regular steak, but it's as close as you'll get while on a gluten-free diet!

Ingredients

For this dish, you will need:
4 large steaks, sliced fairly thin
2 eggs
½ cup of almond flour
1/3 cup of sesame seeds
1/4 cup of flax seeds
Chicken bouillon powder
Basil
Bay leaves
Garlic powder
Salt and black pepper, to taste

Preparation:

To begin, place a pan on the stove to heat, and add in enough oil to deep fry your breaded steak. Let the oil heat as you go about preparing the rest of the meal.

Crack the 2 eggs into a bowl, and beat them vigorously to combine the egg and yolk. Add a pinch of salt into the eggs.

Combine the almond flour, a pinch each of chicken bouillon, garlic powder, salt, and pepper, and the flax seeds in a bowl. Add the sesame seeds into the bowl, and crush three bay leaves in your hands to add them into the mix. Use a fork to stir the dry ingredients together, and make sure that they're properly combined before moving on.

Dip each steak into the eggs, and roll the dipped meat into the flour and seed mixture. Make sure that the entire surface of the meat has been properly coated. If you want to really get the flour coating on right, you can roll the meat in the flour before dipping it into the egg, and roll it a second time after dipping to ensure that the layer of flour is very thick.

Place the steaks in the hot oil one at a time, and cook them until they are golden brown. Remove them from the pan once they are properly cooked, and place them on a plate with paper towels beneath and above them to soak up the oil.

Let the steaks sit until they are all cooked, transfer onto a plate, and serve.

Gluten and Sugar-Free Gingerbread Cake

Want a delicious dessert to make your Christmas celebrations complete? This gluten and sugar-free gingerbread cake will have all of the flavor of the holiday, but with none of the unhealthy nutrients that you're trying to avoid!

Ingredients:

For this cake, you will need:
½ cup of coconut flour
1 cup of amaranth flour
1 cup of buckwheat flour
2 tablespoons of flax meal (For those who want the non-vegan version of this cake, use 2 eggs instead of the flax meal. It will make the cake a bit fluffier, and will help to round out the flavors nicely.)
2 ½ teaspoons of baking soda
Ground cinnamon
Ground ginger
Ground cloves
Ground nutmeg
Salt
Water
¾ cup of agave nectar
¾ cup of molasses

Canola oil
Fresh ginger
Lemon zest

Preparation:

To begin, turn on the oven and let it heat to 350 F. As the oven is heating, prepare the cake.

Combine the coconut flour, amaranth flour, buckwheat flour, and baking soda in a bowl. Add in 2 teaspoons of cinnamon, the same amount of ground ginger, half a teaspoon each of cloves, salt, and nutmeg, and a teaspoon or two of lemon zest. Stir the ingredients well to combine.

In a separate bowl, combine the flax meal with a few tablespoons of water, and stir in the agave, the molasses, ¾ of a cup of canola oil, and a couple of teaspoons of the grated fresh ginger. Mix these ingredients together well, and pour them into the bowl with the dry ingredients. Stir the wet and dry ingredients together to make the batter for the cake, and add about a cup of boiling water to your final batter.

Once the water has been properly mixed in with the rest of the ingredients, pour the cake batter into a buttered baking pan. Place the pan into the oven, and let it cook for about 40 minutes.

You'll find that a toothpick or knife inserted into the center of the cake will come out clean, and it will let you know that your cake is ready to enjoy.

Cut once the cake has cooled a bit, and serve.

Gluten Free Waffles

There's nothing like a heaping stack of waffles to get your morning started the right way, but your regular waffles are loaded with grain and gluten. These delicious grain-free waffles will be the perfect breakfast, and it will help you to enjoy what you're eating without having to worry about adding grain to your diet.

Ingredients

For this dish, you will need:
1 cup of rice flour
1/3 cups of potato starch (not all cornstarch products are gluten-free)
3 tablespoons of tapioca flour
1 ½ teaspoons of baking powder
½ teaspoon of baking soda
Salt
Xanthan gum
Buttermilk
Sugar substitute
2 eggs
Canola oil
2 cups of water

Preparation:

To begin, heat your waffle iron. It takes about 5 to 10 minutes for the waffle iron to heat -- depending on the brand -- so make sure that it's heating as you go about preparing the waffles.

Mix the rice flour, potato starch, tapioca flour, baking soda, and baking powder together in a bowl. Add in about half a teaspoon of salt, and the same amount of xanthan gum. Mix the dry ingredients together, and be sure that they are properly combined before moving on to the next step.

Crack the two eggs into another bowl, and add in the water. Add about 3 tablespoons of the oil, and mix the ingredients together well. Stir them in with the dry ingredients, and mix until you get the waffle batter you want. The batter will be a bit thick, so add buttermilk to produce the desired consistency for the waffle batter. Make sure that there are no lumps.

Use some spray cooking oil to grease the waffle iron, or use regular oil on a paper towel to cover the iron with a thin layer of oil. Pour the batter into the heated iron, and close the lid. Watch the waffle iron until the light turns off, and use a fork to remove the cooked waffle from the waffle maker.

Serve while hot, and enjoy the delicious, crunchy waffles!

Buckwheat Pancakes

For those of you who just can't stay away from those flapjacks, this pancake recipe will be the perfect grain-free solution for you! You'll still be able to have a tall stack of delicious pancakes, but without worrying about gluten or grain.

Ingredients

For this dish, you will need:
1 ½ cups of buckwheat flour
3 tablespoons of sugar (use sugar alternative for a low-sugar meal)
Salt
1 teaspoon of baking soda
Unsalted butter
1 egg
Buttermilk

Preparation:

To begin, place a frying pan on the stove to heat. Make sure that it has been properly heated before placing the batter onto the pan, so give it time to warm up as you make the pancakes.

Mix the flour, sugar, and baking soda together in a bowl. Add in about a teaspoon of salt. Stir the ingredients well to combine.

Crack your egg in another bowl, and beat to combine the yolk and white.

Melt the butter in a saucepan or the microwave, and pour the melted butter over the flour mixture -- stirring as you pour. Add the egg into the mix, and pour in about a cup of buttermilk as well. Stir the batter together, and you'll have a fairly thick mixture. Keep pouring in buttermilk until your pancakes have reached the desired consistency, and stir to ensure that there are no lumps.

Once the batter has been prepared, pour it into a pitcher or an empty ketchup bottle. Gently pour or squeeze the batter onto your heated pan, which you will have coated with a bit of oil to butter to prevent the pancakes from sticking.

Cook until the top of the pancake is riddled with bubbles, and flip it over to cook on the other side for about 20 seconds.

Once the batter has been used up, you'll have a delicious stack of healthy buckwheat pancakes that are grain-free and fairly low calorie!

Grain-Free Cornbread

You can't have chili beans without some delicious cornbread, and there are so many other dishes that won't be complete without this delicious savory baked bread. Don't worry about it being high in grain, as we've substituted the ingredients in the bread for grain-free ones!

Ingredients

For this dish, you will need:
1 ½ cups of cornmeal
1 cup of millet flour
1 cup of rice flour
2 eggs
Water
Vegetable oil
¼ cup of sugar
1 tablespoon of baking powder
Salt

Preparation:

To begin, heat your oven to about 400 degrees. This way, it will be hot enough to cook the bread, but it won't be so hot that the bread will burn.

Use a bit of butter to grease a 9x9 baking dish, and set it aside as you prepare the bread.

In a bowl, crack and beat the eggs vigorously to combine the yolk and egg white. Heat 1 ½ cups of water until they are lukewarm, and add them into the eggs. Drop in ¼ cup of canola or vegetable oil, and mix the ingredients well until they are properly blended.

In a separate bowl, mix the millet flour, rice flour, and cornmeal together. Add in the white sugar, the baking powder, and about a teaspoon of salt. Make sure that the dry ingredients are all mixed together properly, and hollow out a hole in the center of the bowl.

Pour the wet ingredients into the hollowed center of the flour mixture, and use a whisk to stir the ingredients together properly. Whisk and stir until you are sure that there are no lumps, which could take a few minutes.

Once you're sure there are no lumps, pour the batter into the greased baking pan. Place the pan into the oven, and let it cook for about 20 minutes. You can tell that it's cooked by pressing on the surface of the bread. If it's properly done, the corn bread will spring back up when you press gently on it.

Remove from the oven, let the cornbread cool for a few minutes, and serve while still warm.

Curried Quinoa

This delicious side dish is made without any grain, which means that you can eat it whenever you want! The quinoa is a much lower-calorie alternative to rice, but it will be a delicious alternative that will make the dish absolutely fantastic!

Ingredients:

For this dish, you will need:
1 cup of quinoa
Olive oil
1 onion
Garlic
2 cups of chicken broth
Curry powder
Ancho chili powder
Salt and pepper

Preparation:

To begin, place a skillet on the stove to heat. Bring it to medium heat, and pour a couple of tablespoons of olive oil into the pan.

Chop the onion very finely, and add between 3 and 5

cloves of garlic -- depending on your flavor preference. Cook the aromatics in the oil, leaving them in the pan for about 5 minutes to ensure that you have extracted the flavor from them. Add the quinoa into the pan, and cook the seed in the oil until it is lightly toasted.

Once you're done cooking the quinoa, pour the chicken broth into the pan. Cover the pan, and let the broth heat until it begins to boil. Stir in about a tablespoon each of the curry powder and Mexican chili powder, and cover the pan once again.

Turn the heat down to let the quinoa simmer, and let it cook on low heat for about 25 minutes. The quinoa should be soft and tasty, and you can add a bit of salt and pepper to add the flavor you want for the dish. (Serve as the starch with nearly any protein, and it will be a delicious companion for your meal!)

Roasted Almond Cookies

Want to enjoy a delicious dessert without getting into the grain-loaded cookie jar? These cookies are quick and easy to make, and you'll find that they're the perfect grain-free solution to help you stay true to your gluten-free diet!

Ingredients:

For this dish, you will need:
1 cup of raw almonds
½ cup of maple syrup
1 cup of oat flour
Almond extract

Preparation:

Preheat the oven to about 275 F, which will be hot enough to toast the almonds.

Place the cup of almonds onto a baking sheet, and put them in the oven. Let them heat until they become golden brown and are releasing a delightful scent, which will take about 40 minutes. Be careful that they don't burn.

Once the almonds are cooked, remove them from the oven and set them aside to cool. After they have cooled down enough, run them through your food processor to produce a fine almond flour.

Mix the flour in a bowl together with the oat flour, maple syrup, and almond extract.

Turn the heat of the oven up to 350 F, and let it heat.

As the oven is heating, use your hands to form the dough into 6 balls. Press the balls gently to flatten them a bit, until they are about half an inch thick. Place the cookies onto a greased baking sheet, and put the sheet in the oven.

Let the cookies bake for about 12 minutes, but keep a close eye on them because the edges can burn very quickly. They will become browned and crisp around the edges of the cookie, and that's how you'll know that they're done.

Remove them from the oven, let them cool, and enjoy!

Grain-Free Zucchini Bread

Most people think of banana bread or carrot cake as being the only vegetable-laden desserts that you can make, but you'll find that zucchini bread will be a delicious alternative that will be just as healthy and tasty! Thanks to the grain-free recipe, you won't have to worry about the gluten.

Ingredients:

For this dish, you will need:
1 cup of teff flour
1 cup of buckwheat flour
Baking soda
Salt
Baking powder
3 eggs
Lemon zest
Cinnamon
1 cup of apple sauce
½ cup of maple syrup
Coconut oil
Vanilla extract
2 cups of grated zucchini
1 cup of raisins and almonds mixed

Preparation:

To begin, turn on your oven and pre-heat it to about 350 degrees. As it's heating, move on to the next step.

Mix the buckwheat and teff flours together in a bowl, and add in a tablespoon of cinnamon, a teaspoon of salt and lemon zest each, 2 teaspoons of the baking soda, and ¼ teaspoon of baking powder. Stir well to ensure that the ingredients are properly combined before moving on.

In a separate bowl, combine the apple sauce and maple syrup together, and crack the three eggs into the bowl. Beat well to mix the ingredients, and add two teaspoons of vanilla extract and a tablespoon of coconut oil into the bowl. Stir well to mix.

Once the wet ingredients are properly mixed, pour the dry ingredients into the bowl. Stir well or use an electric mixer to combine the ingredients, and stir until there are no more lumps. Pour the zucchini into the batter, and add the raisins and almonds as well. Mix to distribute these ingredients.

Pour the batter into a greased baking pan, which should have a bit of butter along the bottom to help make the cake tasty. Put the pan into the oven, and let it cook for about 50 minutes. The cake will take longer to cook than your average flour cake, but you'll know that it's done when a toothpick or knife inserted into the center of the cake comes out clean.

Remove the cake from the oven, let cool for a few minutes, cut, and serve!

Apple Cobbler

Not quite the same as Apple Crumble, this Apple Cobbler recipe is the perfect grain-free breakfast treat! It will be crunchy, flavorful, and delightful, but it won't have any of the gluten that you're trying so hard to avoid.

Ingredients

For this dish, you will need:
6 apples
1 can of cranberry sauce
Brown sugar
1 cup of steel-cut oats
Cinnamon
Soy milk
Butter

Preparation:

To begin, peel and cut the apples. You will want to make them small slices, easy enough to fit into your mouth without being too small.

Preheat the oven to about 350 F once the apples are done. Grease a baking tray with a bit of butter, and set it aside as you move on.

Combine the apples and the cranberry sauce in a bowl, and add in 2 or 3 tablespoons of the brown sugar. Add ¼ cup of soy milk, and mix the ingredients well to ensure that they are properly combined.

Melt a bit of butter on the stove, and pour the butter over the top of the oats. Toss the oats to coat them evenly with the butter.

Place the apple mixture into the pan, and cover it with a top layer of oats. Place the pan into the oven, and let it cook for about 35 or 40 minutes. You'll see that the oats turn a pleasant golden brown, and the juices released by the apple and cranberry sauce will bubble nicely.

Remove from the oven, let cool for a few minutes, and serve as the perfect healthy breakfast!

Breakfast Cereal Sans Gluten

A healthy breakfast cereal can be the perfect thing to get your morning started the right way, as it will provide you with slow-burning carbs that will give you energy all day long. This breakfast cereal will be perfect, as it comes without grain and will give you that energy boost you need for the long day ahead.

Ingredients:

For this dish, you will need:
½ cup of quinoa
½ cup of buckwheat groats
1 cup of brown basmati rice
½ cup of millet
½ cup of flax seeds
½ cup of sesame seeds
½ cup of cornmeal
½ cup of amaranth

Preparation:

To begin, place the basmati rice into a blender or grinder, and grind until you have produced a coarse rice flour. Empty the rice into a bowl.

Grind or blend all of the other ingredients, and you will end up with a mixture of various flours -- none of which will be wheat or grain flour, of course.

To prepare the cereal, put 4 cups of water into a pan to boil on the stove. Once the water is boiling, add in about a cup of the cereal mixture and a pinch of salt. Add a tablespoon or two of milk powder, and let the ingredients cook until they have thickened.

To add some flavor, add in a bit of cinnamon, some butter, and a tablespoon of sugar. You'll find that these ingredients will sweeten the cereal, and a bit of milk will help to make it more edible.

The cereal mixture will take about 20 minutes to cook, and you should keep the heat low to prevent it from burning. After 20 minutes has passed, scoop into a bowl, let cool for a minute, and enjoy!

Rice Stuffing

Need to stuff that Thanksgiving turkey but don't want to use bread? This rice turkey or chicken stuffing will be the perfect thing for you! It's tasty, subtle, and easy to make, and it will enable you to give your turkey the right filling.

Ingredients:

For this dish, you will need:
2 cups of white rice
Water
Chicken bouillon
1 onion
Butter
Garlic
1 celery stalk
Parsley
Salt
Sage
Thyme
Pepper, to taste

Preparation:

To begin, you will need to dice the onions as fine as you can. Make sure to chop the onions very small.

Place a pot on the stove to heat, and add about a tablespoon of butter into the bottom of the pan. Once the butter has melted, add the onions into the mixture. Let the onions fry for a minute, and chop the garlic as you do so. Add about 5 cloves of garlic -- chopped fine -- into the pan, and fry the garlic along with the onions.

Once the onions have begun to brown around the edges, add the uncooked rice into the pan. You will want to cook the rice until it shows signs of beginning to burn, and the grains will become slightly browned. At this point, add the 2 cups of water into the pan, and cover it.

Once the rice begins to simmer, add a tablespoon or two of chicken bouillon into the pan. Dice the celery stalk, and drop the pieces into the pan. Sprinkle parsley, salt, sage, thyme, and all the pepper you want into the rice.

The simmering water will cook the rice in about 20 minutes, but keep a close eye on it. once the level of the rice rises above the water level, you only have about 5 to 7 more minutes until the rice is completely cooked.

Make sure the rice doesn't burn, and don't let it cook all the way. The rice should still be a bit crunchy when you turn it off.

Once the rice is cooked, remove it from the pan, let it cool, and use it to stuff your turkey. The partially cooked rice will finish cooking as the turkey cooks, and it will come out soft and fluffy!

Gluten Free Irish Shortbread

There's nothing like a good piece of Irish shortbread to eat after your Irish beef stew, and you'll find that a hearty piece of this bread will go down nicely. The best part about this bread: it's made without gluten or wheat!

Ingredients

For this dish, you will need:
2 cups of butter
2 cups of rye flour
1 cup of corn flour
2 cups of brown sugar

Preparation:

To begin, heat the oven to 300 degrees. Take the time to grease two baking pans, or use grease paper to prevent a mess.

Soften the butter in a double boiler, or leave it at room temperature for an hour to make it easier to mash. Use a fork to mix the sugar into the butter, and combine it until it is creamy and blended. Add the corn flour and the rye flour, and combine into a nice dough.

Divide the dough that you have into two portions, and press each portion of dough into the pans that you have prepared. Use the fork to prick some shallow holes, dividing the bread into individual portions. You can sprinkle a bit of sugar to make it decorative.

Place the baking pans into the oven, and let them cook for about an hour. You'll find that the bread can cook in as little time as 45 minutes, so keep an eye on it. You may notice that the edges of the bread are getting browned, and the top will be nicely golden.

Cut the bread into individual pieces while it is still warm, and enjoy!

Asian Sesame Noodles

If you love the taste of the Orient, this will definitely be the dish for you. These tasty noodles are grain-free, but they're absolutely delightful! With the right ingredients added to this dish, you'll have everything you need to get your Oriental on!

Ingredients

For this dish, you will need:
400 grams of Gluten-free noodles
Sesame oil
2 carrots
Garlic
Fresh ginger root
1 onion
½ head of cabbage
½ pepper
1 sprig of cilantro
Almond butter
Gluten-free soy sauce

Preparation:

To begin, you'll need to put a pot of water on the stove to boil. Add about 3 cups of water per 100 grams of noodles, and give it a few minutes to boil.

As the water is heating up, dice the ginger, garlic, and onions. You can use as much garlic as you want, but add no more than a teaspoon of fresh ginger root. Julienne the carrots, the bell pepper, and the cabbage, making the slices as thin as possible.

Place a wok on the stove to heat, and pour in a few tablespoons of sesame oil. Once the oil is hot, drop in the ginger, garlic, and onions. Stir fry the ingredients for a few minutes, and add in the carrots. Once the carrots have begun to soften, add in the peppers and the cabbage. Cook for just 3 minutes, and add the soy sauce into the mixture.

Place the noodles in the water to cook, and keep a close eye on them. You don't want them to overcook, as they'll be quite unpleasant. Make sure that they're al dente, and remove them from the stove. Drain the water, run cold water over the noodles, and throw the noodles into the wok.

Stir fry the noodles with the other ingredients, adding a tablespoon of almond butter, 2 tablespoons of soy sauce, and ½ tablespoon of sesame oil to flavor the noodles. Cook until the liquid has all been eliminated from the wok, leaving you with a dry, slightly fried noodle dish.

Serve the noodles onto two plates, chop the cilantro to sprinkle on top of the noodles, and serve with chopsticks and your favorite Chinese hot sauce.

Shrimp Cakes

Want to enjoy some seafood, but can't eat gluten? These gluten-free shrimp cakes are an absolute delight, and they'll help you to get a lot more protein in your diet. They're fairly easy to make, but they're definitely a delicious meal that will be ideal for anyone on a weight loss diet.

Ingredients

For this dish, you will need:
1 pound of shrimp
1 red bell pepper
2 cloves of garlic
Scallions
Lime juice
Sea salt
Chipotle
1 egg
½ cup of almond flour
Grapeseed or peanut
½ cup of chopped cilantro

Preparation:

To begin, peel and de-vein the shrimp. This can be a lengthy process, so be prepared to spend at least 20 minutes in this activity.

Once the shrimp has been prepared, throw them into the blender or food processor. Press the pulse button until the shrimp has been chopped fine, and remove the shrimp from the blender.

Pour the shrimp into a bowl, and add a teaspoon of sea salt, the cilantro, and ¼ teaspoon of chipotle. Crack the egg into the bowl, and mix it well to combine.

Dice the scallions, the garlic, and the bell pepper, making sure that they are very finely chopped. Add them into the bowl, and stir to mix properly. Add the lime juice for the finishing flavor touches.

Use your hands to form the ingredients into balls, which you will dip into the almond flour to coat them thoroughly as you flatten them into patties.

Place a skillet on the stove to heat, and add enough oil to fry the patties. Place four of the patties into the skillet at a time, and cook for about 5 minutes. Turn the patty onto its other side, and cook it until that side is also browned.

Remove the cooked patties from the pan, and place them on a paper towel to drain as you cook the rest. You should obtain about 12 patties from this mixture.

Enjoy with a simple marinara sauce, or just pour some of your favorite hot sauce over the patties to make them taste delicious!

Stuffed Bell Peppers

This dish is made with a rice stuffing that will be absolutely divine, not to mention free of gluten. If you want to enjoy a delicious stuffed bell pepper, this is a recipe that you must try!

Ingredients:

For this dish, you will need:
6 green bell peppers
Diced green chilies
1 pound of ground beef
1 onion
5 cloves of garlic
1 cup of rice
Cumin
Cilantro
Chili powder
Sea salt

Preparation:

To begin, place a pan on the stove to heat. Pour a tablespoon of oil into the bottom of the pan, and dice one of the cloves of garlic. Cook the garlic until it's nicely browned, and add the rice into the pan. Once the rice is toasted, pour 1 cup of water into the pan. Cover it and cook on low heat until the rice is done. Remove from the heat and set aside.

Dice the onion and the rest of the garlic very finely, and place a skillet on the stove to heat. With a bit of oil in the bottom of the pan, sauté the garlic and onions for a few minutes. Add the ground beef into the pan, and cook it until it's well done. Add ½ can of diced green chilies 3 minutes before the meat is done, and cook them with the meat. Once you have turned off the meat, add in a teaspoon of cumin, ½ cup of diced fresh cilantro, a teaspoon of chili powder, and a tablespoon of sea salt.

Take the ground beef mixture and add it into the pan with the rice. Mix well to combine, and add salt and pepper as desired.

Use a knife to score around the top of the bell pepper, and pull off the top to extract the seeds. Wash the peppers thoroughly to remove any remaining seeds.

Heat the oven to 350 F.

Use a spoon to scoop the rice and beef mixture into the bell peppers, stuffing them completely full. Remove the seeds from the tops of the bell peppers, and place the tops back on the peppers. Place the bell peppers on a tray, and place the tray in the oven.

Let the peppers cook for about 45 minutes to an hour, and they will be ready to eat!

Gluten-Free Turkey Club

This is a delicious sandwich that you can make all on your own, and you'll be able to use gluten-free bread to slap together this quick and easy meal. You can used gluten-free bread that you bought from the store, or you can make your own loaf of gluten-free nut bread. This recipe will just tell you how to make the perfect sandwich, but there's a recipe further down that will tell you how to make the bread.

Ingredients

For this dish, you will need:
3 slices of gluten-free bread
4 slices of turkey ham
1 avocado
2 slices of your favorite cheese
Onion
Tomato
Canned chipotle chili peppers
Lettuce
Pickles
Alfalfa sprouts
Dijon mustard
Tabasco sauce
Light mayonnaise

Preparation:

To begin, place a skillet on the stove to heat. Once the skillet is properly hot, place the bread on the skillet. Only toast one side of two slices of bread, but toast the third slice on both sides.

Remove the bread from the skillet, and start with one of the half-toasted slices placed toasted side down.

Onto this slice of bread, spread a bit of mayonnaise. Add 2 slices of turkey, one slice of cheese, 1 onion ring, two pickles, and the alfalfa sprouts. Sprinkle Tabasco sauce generously. Grab the fully toasted slice of bread, and spread Dijon mustard on one side and mayo on the other. Place the toast mustard side down on top of the other ingredients.

Add the last two slices of turkey onto the sandwich, along with the cheese, 1 slice of tomato, 1 diced canned chipotle pepper, 3 slices of avocado, and two leaves of lettuce. Sprinkle Tabasco sauce generously onto the sandwich, and spread Dijon mustard onto the untoasted side of the final piece of bread before completing your sandwich.

Cut in half, serve, and enjoy!

All Purpose, Gluten and Grain-Free Nut Bread

This is the nut bread that you can use to make sandwiches, cheese toast, eat with your morning coffee, or just snack on when you're hungry. It's a gluten and grain-free bread that you can use for just about anything, and it will be the perfect option regardless of what sweet or savory dish you need bread for. It's also quick and easy to make!

Ingredients:

For this dish, you will need:
¼ cup of flax meal
1 ½ cups of almond flour
Salt
4 eggs
½ teaspoon of baking soda
1 cup of walnuts, hazelnuts, almonds, and other nuts.
¼ cup of sesame seeds
¼ cup of amaranth
¼ cup of sunflower seeds
1 teaspoon of apple cider vinegar
1 teaspoon of agave honey

Preparation:

To begin, heat the oven to about 350 F, and grease two bread pans.

Combine the almond flour with the flax meal, baking soda, and a pinch of salt in a bowl, stirring well to ensure that the ingredients are properly combined.

Crack the eggs into a bowl, and use a fork or whisk to beat them well. Make sure they are frothy, and add into the bowl the agave honey and vinegar. Mix the wet and dry ingredients together in a bowl, and add the various nuts and seeds into the same bowl. Use a fork or whisk to mix the ingredients properly until there are no lumps.

Pour the bread batter into the greased bread pans, and put them in the oven. The bread will probably take about 30 to 40 minutes to cook, so keep an eye on them. Check the bread for doneness by inserting a knife into the center, and it will come out clean when it's done cooking.

Remove from the oven, set aside to cool, and slice the bread once it has reached room temperature. You now have the ideal loaf of bread for just about anything!

Pad Thai

Pad Thai is one of the most popular Thai dishes in the country, and it will be a wonderful grain-free alternative to the more popular Chinese and Japanese fried noodle dishes. It's fairly easy to make, and it's absolutely delicious!

Ingredients

For this dish, you will need:
6 ounces of rice noodles
Sesame oil
1 onion
1 head of broccoli
Water
4 cloves of garlic
Scallions
Cilantro
Peanuts
Salt and pepper, to taste

Preparation:

To begin, place a pot of water on the stove to boil. Bring the water to a boil, and drop the rice noodles in to cook. The package will usually have clear instructions on how to cook the noodles, so follow them precisely for al dente noodles. Drain the noodles, run cold water over them, and set them aside.

Place a skillet on the stove to heat, and add a bit of sesame oil into the bottom. Dice the onion very fine, and add it into the pan to be sautéed. Cook the onions on medium-low heat, and make sure they are nicely browned.

As the onions are cooking, cut the broccoli into bite-sized spears. Once about 10 minutes has passed, add the broccoli in with the browned onions. Add ¼ cup of water, and cover the pan. Let the broccoli sauté with the onions for roughly 5 minutes, after which time it will become soft and turn a bright color.

Add salt to the pan, and dice the garlic to be added as well. Add a bit more sesame oil to ensure that the ingredients don't dry out, and add some diced peanuts into the pan. Use a tablespoon of arrowroot powder and water to thicken the mixture, and stir fry the ingredients to ensure that the powder is spread all around.

Place the noodles onto a plate, and pour the vegetable mixture over the top. If you want to add some protein, throw some shrimp into a pan and grill them to serve on top of the vegetables and noodles.

Garnish with some scallions and diced cilantro, and enjoy!

Gluten-Free Chicken Noodle Soup

There's nothing like a cup of chicken noodle soup when you're feeling ill, but wheat noodles would just make the problem worse. With this grain-free chicken noodle soup, you'll always feel better, and it is a tasty soup that you can't help but love!

Ingredients:

For this dish, you will need:
1 liter of chicken broth
1 stalk of celery
1 onions
3 cloves of garlic
1 carrot
1 zucchini
1 pack of gluten-free noodles
½ chicken breast

Preparation:

To begin, dice the onions and the carrots very finely. Make sure that they are diced very small.

Place a pot on the stove to heat, and drop a tablespoon of olive oil into the bottom. Add the garlic and onions into the pot, and sauté them until they are browned.

Once the onions and garlic are properly cooked, add the chicken broth into the pot. Set the heat on medium, and let the broth boil.

As the broth is heating up, cut the carrots into small pieces about as large as your fingernails. Throw them into the pot, along with the celery - which you will slice into small pieces as well.

Run the zucchini through a julienne slicer, and you'll have what looks like simple noodles. Put them into the pot, and let them cook along with the other ingredients.

On the side, add a bit of butter into a skillet. Slice the chicken breast into small chunks, and cook the chicken in the pot until browned on the outside. Add the partially cooked chicken into the pot of soup, ensuring that you get all the liquid and oil from the skillet.

Turn the soup up to high heat, and let it cook for another 15 minutes. Once that time has passed, drop the gluten-free soup noodles into the mixture, and let them cook on low heat. Once the noodles have cooked properly, turn off the fire and remove the pot from the stove.

Serve, add a splash of lime, and enjoy!

Gluten-Free Potato Beef Stew

Want to make a thick, hearty stew without adding flour or wheat to the mixture? This delicious stew will be an ideal meal to have on a cold winter evening, and it will be just as rich and hearty as any stew made with flour to thicken it!

Ingredients:

For this dish, you will need:
4 potatoes
1 pound of stew meat
2 carrots
1 onion
5 cloves of garlic
½ cup of table wine
¼ cup of soy sauce
1 cup of milk
2 liters of beef broth
Salt and pepper, to taste
Preparations:

To begin, peel one potato, dice it, and place it in a small pot of water to boil. Let the potato cook for about an hour, adding more water into the pot whenever necessary. Once the potato has cooked for the prescribed 60 minutes, drain all but the final dregs of water, mash with a fork, and set aside.

Place a soup pot on the stove to heat, along with a couple of tablespoons of peanut oil in the bottom of the pot.

Dice the onion and the garlic, and add them into the pot to sauté. Add the onions first, and let them cook until nearly browned before adding in the garlic.

Dice the stew meat into small bite-sized pieces, and add them into the pot once the garlic has been properly cooked. Cook the meat until it has been browned on the outside, and add the beef broth into the pot. Bring the beef broth to a boil as you cut the other vegetables.

Cut the potatoes into medium-sized cubes, and add them into the pot. Peel and cut the potatoes into slices, and add them into the pot.

Let the stew boil for about 20 minutes, or until you're sure the potatoes are nearly cooked. Add in the soy sauce, table wine, and the milk, and let it keep cooking. Add salt and pepper as desired, along with crushed bay leaves for added flavor.

Just 5 minutes before you are about to turn the soup off, add in the mashed potato. Stir the soup well, ensuring that the mashed potato is diluted properly. The starch from the potato will thicken the stew, but it will ensure that the other ingredients aren't overcooked.

Serve with nut bread, and enjoy!

Grain-Free Ideal Breakfast

The ideal way to start the day is with a rich breakfast, but the average breakfast consists of grain-laden toast, pancakes, or other things that are made with grain. If you want the perfect breakfast without adding grain to your diet, this is the recipe for you!

Ingredients:

For this dish, you will need:
3 eggs
2 slices of turkey or Canadian bacon
6 oranges
2 Slices of Nut bread (see recipe above)
Butter
Honey
Coffee

Preparation:

To begin, place a skillet on the stove to heat. Once the skillet is hot, add the bacon and cook until done. Remove the bacon from the stove, and place on a paper towel to drain.

Leaving the bacon grease in the bottom of the pan, let it

reheat until ready for the eggs. Crack one egg into the pan, and crack the other two eggs into a cup -- making sure to get only the egg whites. Add the two egg whites into the pan, and cook the eggs until done as desired. (If you don't like your eggs to be liquid on the top, flip them over and let them sit in the pan for 3 seconds before scooping them onto your plate.)

Add the slices of nut bread onto the plate, along with the Canadian or turkey bacon. Spread butter and honey as desired on the bread, and serve yourself a cup of coffee.

Squeeze the oranges, and enjoy your fresh cup of OJ for the ideal grain-free breakfast!

Dark Chicken Soup

If you're not too particular about the way your soup looks, you'll find that this will be the ideal meal for you! It comes loaded with all the nutrients you need, and there are even a few noodles floating around to help fill you up. All in all, however, it's a nicely low calorie meal - and grain-free as well!

Ingredients

For this dish, you will need:
2 liters of chicken broth
1 bunch of chard
2 carrots
1 bunch of spinach
1 cup of shitake mushrooms
1 pack of shitake mushroom noodles
¼ pound of chicken breast

Preparation:

To begin, place the chard and spinach in a pot with 2 cups of water and 2 cups of chicken stock. Bring the veggies to a boil, and let them cook until they are soft. Pour the soup into the food processor, blend it until it is completely liquefied, and set it aside.

Pour the chicken broth into a pot, and bring it to a boil. Cut the carrots and shitake mushrooms into slices, and add them into the soup. Pour the liquefied dark greens into the pot, and let them cook along with the chicken broth.

In a pan on the side, add a pat of butter into the bottom as the pan heats. Dice the chicken breast into chunks, and let the breast cook until it is browned on the outside. Once it is nearly cooked, pour the chicken and the grease into the soup pot. Let it cook until you're sure the chicken is thoroughly done.

Add the mushroom noodles a few minutes before you want to cook the soup, and follow the cooking instructions on the package. The noodles shouldn't take too long to cook, and you can serve out the soup while it's still piping hot!

Carrot Muffins

These delicious muffins will help you to start the day out right, and you can munch on a couple of them as you head to work. Thanks to the fact that they're completely grain-free, they'll be the perfect option for you!

Ingredients

For this dish, you will need:
¼ teaspoon of baking soda
¼ cup of coconut flour
Cinnamon
3 eggs
Salt
¼ cup of oil
¼ cup of natural molasses
Vanilla
3 carrots
¼ cup of raspberries, blackberries, and black currants

Preparation:

To begin, preheat the oven to about 350 F. This is the perfect temperature for muffins, as it will keep cooking time down without risking burning the muffins.

Combine the baking soda, coconut flour, and a teaspoon of cinnamon in a bowl, and stir it well to ensure that it's properly combined.

In a separate bowl, crack and mix the eggs. Whip them until they are frothy, and pour the oil, molasses, and a teaspoon of vanilla into the mix. Beat well, add a pinch of salt, and combine the wet ingredients with the dry.

Use a whisk to combine the wet and dry ingredients well, and stir until you are sure there are no lumps.

With a bit of butter, grease a muffin tray. You'll get about 12 to 18 medium-sized muffins, though as many as 30 mini muffins. Put the tray into the oven, and cook the muffins for about 30 minutes. Insert a knife into the top of one muffin, and it should come out clean once it's done.

Remove the muffins from the oven, scoop them out of their tray, and set them aside to cool.

Almond and Grilled Chicken Salad

The beauty of salads is that they are some of the best grain-free recipes, and you won't have to worry about getting gluten if you eat a healthy salad. If you want to really go all out with the salad, add nuts and lots of filling veggies! You'll find that it will be tasty and very enjoyable!

Ingredients:

For this dish, you will need:
1 pound of chicken breast
1 head of Romaine or Iceberg lettuce
1 cup of raw almonds
1 cup of raw peanuts
1 cup of dried cranberries
1 apple
½ cup of olive oil
½ cup of apple cider vinegar
1 cup of gluten-free soy sauce
Salt
Sesame seeds

Preparation:

To begin, slice the chicken breast into steaks about ¾ inch thick. You'll get about 3 steaks from a single chicken breast. Place the chicken breast on a grill, and rub a seasoning of salt, pepper, garlic, and Parmesan cheese onto the breast before cooking it. Grill the chicken well on both sides, and make sure that the middle of the chicken is cooked before removing it from the grill. Set the chicken aside.

Soak the lettuce in a bowl of ice cold water, which will make it crunchy and crispy. Once the lettuce has soaked for 30 minutes, use your hands to rip it into bite-sized leaves.

Slice the apple into quarters, cut out the cores, and cut the apple into small chunks. Add the apples into the salad, along with the cranberries.

In a skillet on the stove, place the almonds and peanuts together. The raw nuts will need to be toasted, and they will take about 20 minutes. Make sure to stir them every 5 minutes or so, and keep the heat on medium high to prevent them from burning. Once the almonds and peanuts are toasted, add them into the salad.

Slice the chicken breast into strips, and add them into the salad as well.

Combine the vinegar, soy sauce, and olive oil together, along with a pinch of salt and some black pepper. Pour this mixture over the salad, and sprinkle sesame seeds liberally on top to garnish the salad. It's now ready for you to eat!

Gluten-Free Breakfast Biscuits

There's nothing like a delicious, buttery biscuit to start your day off on the right foot, and these grain-free biscuits will be just what you need to enjoy your morning. They're easy to whip up, and you can take them with you to snack in your car on the way to work.

Ingredients

For this dish, you will need:
2 cups of almond flour
½ teaspoon of baking soda
2 eggs
1 teaspoon of honey
1/3 cup of butter or margarine
Salt

Preparation:

To begin, preheat the oven to about 350 F. This is the temperature that will allow the biscuits to turn golden brown on the outside, but without making the center of the biscuits too dry.

In a bowl, combine the almond flour with the baking soda and a pinch of salt. Stir well to ensure that there are no clumps of baking soda.

In another bowl, crack the eggs and beat them until they are frothy. Add in the butter and the honey, and beat well. You'll want to keep stirring until you have a slightly creamy mixture.

Fold the wet ingredients gently into the dry ones, and mix until you're sure that there are no lumps. You will need to keep stirring as the dough is formed.

Use a piece of greased baking paper to roll the biscuit dough out, and keep rolling until you've flattened the dough to about 1 ½ inches thick. Use a jar with a wide mouth to cut out the biscuits, and keep rolling the dough until you have turned it all into biscuits.

Transfer the biscuits to an oven tray with a piece of greased baking paper, and put the tray into the oven. Let the biscuits cook for about 15 minutes, and keep a close eye on them. You'll notice that the rounded edges of the biscuits will start to brown, and don't let them get too dark before removing them from the oven.

Use a spatula to scrape the biscuits off the greased baking sheet, and set them on a rack to cool. Once they're cool, spread a bit of butter and honey on them, and enjoy!

Nutty Granola

Granola is one of the best breakfasts that you can have, and you'll find that this nutty granola will be just the thing to stoke up your internal furnace first thing in the morning. It's a grain-free breakfast that will kick off your day in style!

Ingredients

For this dish, you will need:
1 cup of steel cut oats
2 cups of almonds
1 cup of amaranth
1 cup of raisins
1 cup of walnuts
1 tablespoon of vanilla
Butter
Cinnamon
Sugar

Preparation:

To begin, place a skillet on the stove to heat. Melt a cup of butter in the bottom of the skillet, and add the oats in once the butter is liquefied completely.

Use a spatula or wooden spoon to roll the oats thoroughly in the butter, and ensure that the oats are properly coated. Remove the skillet from the heat, and transfer the oats into a flat baking tray.

Preheat the oven to 350 F.

Add the raisins into the oats, and cut the almonds and walnuts in half. Add in the amaranth, and sprinkle a bit of sugar, cinnamon, and a few tablespoons of vanilla extract onto the oats. Make sure that the oats are mixed properly, and put the tray into the oven to cook.

Give the oats about 30 minutes to cook at 350 F, but keep checking them to ensure that they don't burn. You'll find that they'll become nice and crunchy once they've cooked properly, but let them cool down before eating them.

Grain-Free Breakfast Bars

Need something quick to munch on as you drive to work in the morning? Don't let the heavy traffic get you down, but make these delicious breakfast bars to help keep your mind off the fact that you're sitting and doing nothing. They're a healthy breakfast that you can enjoy on the go!

Ingredients

For this dish, you will need:
2 cups of almond flour
1/3 teaspoon of baking soda
1/3 cup of grapeseed oil
Vanilla extract
1/3 cup of honey
½ cup of shredded coconut
1/3 cup of raisins
1/3 cup of nuts (your preference)
¼ cup of flax seeds
¼ cup of amaranth
¼ pumpkin seeds

Preparation:

To begin, preheat the oven to 350 F.

In a bowl, combine the almond flour with a pinch of salt and the baking soda. Make sure to mix well, as that will eliminate any lumps of baking soda.

In another bowl, mix the honey with a tablespoon of vanilla and the grapeseed oil. The oil will be a bit hard to mix in, but a bit of effort will yield a properly mixed liquid.

Pour the wet ingredients in with the dry ones, and whisk vigorously to ensure that the wet and dry ingredients combine nicely without any lumps.

Once you're done mixing, add the nuts, seeds, raisins, coconut, and amaranth into the batter. Mix well to distribute the latest additions.

Use a bit of butter to grease the bottom of a baking tray, and pour the mixture into the pan. Place the pan in the oven, and let it cook for about 20 minutes at 350 F. You'll find that it turns a nice golden brown, and it will become very crunchy and a bit hard to cut.

Slice the bars into small pieces, and serve or set aside to eat on the go.

Garden-Style Hot Dogs

Hot dogs are one of the most popular American foods around, but the problem is the hot dog bun. If you want to enjoy a classic hot dog in a very unique way, these garden-style hot dogs will be an ideal way for you to eliminate the gluten from your meal.

Ingredients:

For this dish, you will need:
6 hot dogs
6 slices of bacon
1 head of Romaine lettuce
½ tomato
½ onion
Pickle relish
Sauerkraut
Ketchup
Mayo
Mustard
Tabasco sauce

Preparation:

To begin, soak the head of lettuce in ice cold water. The cold water will help to make the lettuce crunchier and crispier, which will make it much easier to eat.

Place a skillet on the stove, and let it heat. As the pan is heating, wrap one strip of bacon around each hotdog. You can hold the bacon in place using toothpicks, but make sure that the toothpicks don't interfere with the cooking process.

Let the hot dogs cook for about 20 minutes on low heat, and turn them regularly to ensure that they don't burn. The grease from the bacon will make them very tasty.

Once they're thoroughly cooked, remove the skillet from the stove, but leave the hot dogs inside.

Remove 12 strips of lettuce, and make 6 stacks of two leaves. Dice the tomato and the onions, making sure that they are very small.

Place a bit of sauerkraut in **the bottom** layer of lettuce, and stack the second leaf on top. Place each hot dog into the top leaf, and add tomato, onion, and pickle relish on top. Add the condiments of your choice, and enjoy the delicious, all-natural hot dog meal!

Grain-Free Mac and Cheese

Mac and Cheese is the quintessential American meal, but egg noodles are made with wheat. Using gluten-free noodles will allow you to still enjoy this delicious dish, but without having to worry about adding grain to your meal!

Ingredients

For this dish, you will need:
2 packs of gluten-free noodles
3 cups of grated cheddar cheese
½ cup of butter
1 ½ cups of milk
2 tablespoons of heavy cream
¼ pound of bacon
1 onion
4 cloves of garlic

Preparation:

To begin, place a skillet on the stove to heat. Add a bit of butter into the bottom of the skillet, and dice the onions as the pan gets hot. Add the onions into the bottom of the pan to sauté, and dice the garlic to add in once the onions begin to brown.

Remove the garlic and onions from the stove once the aroma of the garlic is extracted, and slice the bacon as the skillet heats up once again. Place a pot of water on the stove to boil, which will be for the noodles.

Once the skillet is hot, add the bacon into the pan. Cook until it is nicely browned, and remove from the stove.

Place the onions and garlic back on the stove, and pour the milk and bacon into the pan. Once the milk gets hot, add in the heavy cream and the butter. Bring the ingredients to a boil, and add the cheddar cheese into the mix. Turn the fire off, but leave the pan on the stove.

Boil the noodles, and cook them until they are al dente. Place the noodles back into the pot they were cooked in, add the cheese sauce over the top, garnish with a bit more cheese, and serve while hot!

Almond Raisin Muffins

These muffins are simple and easy to make, but they'll be delicious without a doubt! You can even top them with icing to make delicious cupcakes, or keep them light if you're on a diet! Enjoy them no matter where you are, as they are fantastic.

Ingredients:

For this dish, you will need:
1 cup of flax meal
1 cup of almond flour
1 tablespoon of baking powder
Nutmeg
Cinnamon
½ cup of raisins
1/3 cup of toasted **almonds**
1 stick of butter
Salt
4 eggs
½ cup of sugar
½ cup of buttermilk
2 tablespoons of brown sugar

Preparation:

To begin, you will need to heat the oven to about 375 F. Once the oven is hot, turn it down to 350 F, which is the ideal temperature for baking the muffins.

Combine the baking powder, flax meal, almond flour, and a pinch of salt in a bowl, mixing well to combine. Add a teaspoon each of cinnamon and nutmeg, and stir well.

Combine the butter, eggs, sugar, and milk in a bowl, and beat until the eggs are frothy and the butter is creamy. Using melted butter will make the process a lot quicker, but you can use an egg beater if you don't want to take the time to melt the butter.

Combine the wet and dry ingredients, and mix them well to eliminate any lumps. Add the raisins into the mix. Chop the toasted almonds into small pieces, and add them into the muffin batter as well.

Once the ingredients are all stirred in well, pour the muffin batter into a muffin baking tray. Use paper muffin cups if you want to limit the mess.

Place the muffins in the oven, and let them cook for

roughly 15 to 20 minutes, depending the altitude of your city(it takes longer for things to bake the higher above sea level you are). Insert a toothpick into the top of the muffins when they look cooked, and they are done when the toothpick comes out clean.

Remove the muffins from the tray, set them aside to cool, and serve.

Grain-Free Pizza

Pizza is one of the most popular dishes in the world, but it's hard to make a good pizza without using flour. This pizza is made without wheat, and it's a tasty alternative that gluten-sensitive people can enjoy without worrying about their stomachs acting up.

Ingredients

For this dish, you will need:

1 cup of quinoa flour
1 cup of potato flour
1 cup of almond flour
1 cup of buckwheat
Salt
Xanthan gum
4 teaspoons of dried yeast
Canola or olive oil
Water
Tomato sauce
Cheese
Pizza toppings of your choice

Preparation:

To begin, heat the oven to a toasty 350 F.

Grease some baking sheets with a bit of olive or canola oil, and place them on the trays where you will be cooking your pizza.

Sift the various flours, salt, and baking soda into a bowl, and combine the dry ingredients well. Add the yeast into the mixture.

Mix half a liter of warm water with a couple of tablespoons of olive oil, and add the wet ingredients into the dry ones. Mix the dough until it is properly combined, and set it aside for a few minutes to rise.

Once it has risen, use a spoon to scoop it into your pizza tray. Make a nicely rounded pizza, and put it in the oven to cook until the crust is golden brown.

All that is left to do is to scoop the pizza or tomato sauce onto the top of the crust, add cheese, and top with the ingredients of your choice. Put the crust back into the oven, and cook it until the cheese has properly melted.

Slice, serve, and enjoy!

Your Grain Free Meal Plan

So, you've got all these awesome grain-free recipes to work with! Whether you're trying to lose weight or just stay healthy, eating these foods will help you to keep grain and gluten out of your life. If you want to add these delicious meals to your diet, here is an 11-day meal plan that you can use to incorporate all of these recipes into your life:

Day 1:
Breakfast: Buckwheat Pancakes
Lunch: Eggs and Nut Bread Toast
Dinner: Pad Thai

Day 2:
Breakfast: Gluten Free Waffles
Lunch: Grain-Free Cornbread with Grilled Chicken or Steak, plus plenty of veggies
Dinner: Special K cereal (made with rice rather than wheat flour)

Day 3:
Breakfast: Special K Cereal
Lunch: Stuffed Bell Peppers
Dinner: Chicken with Rice Stuffing

Dessert: Roasted Almond Cookies

Day 4:
Breakfast: Apple Cobbler
Lunch: Asian Sesame Noodles
Dinner: Almond and Grilled Chicken Salad

Day 5:
Breakfast: Breakfast Cereal Sans Gluten
Lunch: Grain Free Breaded Chicken with Nut Bread and veggies
Dinner: Gluten-Free Chicken Noodle Soup with Nut Bread
Dessert: Gluten and Sugar-Free Gingerbread Cake

Day 6:
Breakfast: Carrot Muffins
Lunch: Gluten-Free Turkey Club
Dinner: Curried Quinoa with Chick Peas

Day 7:
Breakfast: Grain-Free Ideal Breakfast
Lunch: Dark Chicken Soup with Nut Bread
Dinner: Grain-Free Mac and Cheese

Day 8:
Breakfast: Gluten-Free Breakfast Biscuits

Lunch: Gluten-Free Potato Beef Stew
Dinner: Shrimp Cakes
Dessert: Gluten-Free Irish Shortbread

Day 9:
Breakfast: Nutty Granola
Lunch: Dark Chicken Soup with Nut Bread
Dinner: Special K Cereal

Day 10:
Breakfast: Breakfast Bars
Lunch: Garden-Style Hot Dogs
Dinner: Sesame Seed Chicken Fried Steak

Day 11:
Breakfast: Almond Flour Muffins
Lunch: Grain-Free Pizza
Dinner: Special K Cereal

The meal plan above doesn't come with the calorie count on each food item, but that's something that won't be as important as the fact that they are all grain-free foods. You can eat them without worrying too much about calories, but try and keep the consumption of these foods to a healthy minimum in order to avoid gaining weight!

All of these recipes can be found online, though some of them are our own original creations. You can probably find similar recipes on websites like AllRecpes.com, About.com, and particularly ElanasPantry.com. They are all recipes that someone made, and we just wanted to share them with you. We've made a few adjustments to the various recipes so that you'll get only our unique grain-free flavor on the recipes, but you'll find that there are many like them. The important thing is that you can enjoy your grain-free cooking and eating, and we wanted to provide you with a recipe book that you can use to prepare delicious meals free of grain and gluten. We apologize if you've seen these recipes elsewhere, and we hope that you enjoy the creations we have presented to you!

[1] http://www.stuff.co.nz/life-style/38883/The-effects-of-gluten-on-health

Section 2: Comfort Food Diet

Comfort food is meant to bring out a special feeling in all who eat it, as it creates a sense of nostalgia. It reminds us of the days where we would play with our friends from dawn until dusk and mom would have a special meal waiting when we returned home.

For many, these meals remain a comforting reminder of family and everything that it means. These recipes remind us of simpler times where the entire family would gather around the table and all seemed right with the world. In today's society, it can be difficult to find time to make the meals that mom used to make, but there are ways to make the cooking process much easier. Eating comfort food does not mean that you have to spend the entire day slaving over a hot stove, as many of the recipes allow you to cook outstanding and comforting food without sacrificing your entire day.

At the same time, it is important to remember the things that go into creating a healthy diet. Comfort food might not have the best reputation in that regard, but you do not have to eat unhealthily just because you love comfort food. Much of eating healthy has to do with the ingredients that you use and portion control. In past generations, we did not have this information regarding these ingredients, but now we do. Try using organic ingredients whenever possible and substitute low fat items for higher fat items. Of course, there will be situations where you eat a high-fat meal, but do not let that discourage you. After all, you are a human being and you have the unique ability to enjoy your food. This collection of recipes is meant to help you enjoy your meals, without causing you to gain weight.

Another thing to consider is portion control. Many of the meals in this collection are extremely large, but they are not meant to be consumed by a singular person. These meals are meant to be enjoyed by a group of people, as you gather the family together for a special night. They are also meant to leave leftovers, as you will see in the meal plan at the end of the cookbook. If you make larger portions, you will have leftovers for the next day, which can save you money. The more you can avoid eating out at lunch, the more money you will have in your bank account at the end of the month.

Comfort food is created to be enjoyed and by following these great recipes, you can be certain that you will enjoy your meals for years to come.

Chapter 1: Comfort Food – What Is It?

Before you can begin your comfort food diet, it is a good idea to know exactly what you are getting yourself into. Simply put, comfort food is anything that brings about a sense of nostalgia when eating it. As a result, comfort food recipes will be different for everyone, as it is a very personal experience.

When putting together a comfort food diet cookbook, it is important to include recipes from all parts of the country and to represent various ethnic backgrounds. It is equally important to include all-American dishes that everyone who lives in the country has tried or, at the very least, heard of.

If you decide to use these comfort food diet recipes, remember that each one represents the sense of family that you get when sitting around the table over a hot meal. Also remember that when prepared properly, these meals are healthy and nutritious, so you do not have to worry about your comfort foods diet creating health problems in the future. Too much of today's food is based on fad diets that die out over time, but this food lovers diet is sure to stand the test of time.

Comfort Food Breakfasts

Most healthy diets start off with a food breakfast and comfort food is no different. The majority of comfort food breakfasts are hearty and will stick with you throughout the day. Breakfast is extremely important because it helps you keep your energy levels high in the morning. Those who do not get off to a good start with a healthy breakfast tend to fade before lunch, which hinders their productivity at work. Start your day off with a good breakfast and the rest of the day will easily fall into place.

Comfort Food Lunches

When you think of comfort food lunches, the first thing that might come to mind is leftovers from the previous night's dinner. While leftovers can certainly be used as a comfort food lunch, the genre has many options on its own. Hearty soups and sandwiches highlight this healthy food diet, as they provide the nutrients that you need to finish up the day at work as strongly as you started it.

Comfort Food Dinners

Of course, the main meal that is associated with comfort food is dinner, as this is where the family is most likely to get together for a large meal. These meals are meant to be enjoyed by the entire family, with plenty leftover to eat the next day. These are the meals that mom would spend all day cooking, although modern technology means that you can cook these same meals in a fraction of the time. Every time you use this comfort food diet cookbook, you should envision time spent with the ones that you love the most and enjoy every minute of eating these delicious meals.

Comfort Food Desserts

After a huge dinner, it can sometimes be difficult to get through dessert. At the same time, however, you know that the dessert will be delicious and you force yourself to have some of it. While often unnecessary, these desserts are a major part of what makes up this healthy food diet. While not overly filling, most of these desserts provide family members with the time to unwind after a large meal, which gives them the opportunity to spend even more time together.

Bringing People Together

Of course, it is not always possible to bring the family together for a meal, but that should not stop you from looking at these recipes. Some of these recipes are large enough for the entire family, while others are small enough that you can enjoy them on your own. At the end of the day, it is all about how the food makes you feel and every meal in this book should make you feel great after you eat it.

Chapter 2: Comfort Food Breakfast Recipes

Breakfast is the most important meal of the day and if you skip it, you could end up without the energy that you need to get through the morning. Comfort food is often associated with large meals, but many of them are also very quickly to make. By making a quick breakfast in the morning, you can save yourself from feeling weak later on in the day. You can also prevent yourself from overeating in the afternoon, which makes this sort of a comfort foods diet. When you choose diet comfort food for breakfast, you give yourself a great chance of losing weight, without going hungry.

Another thing to consider is that some of these recipes can be eaten on the road. If you take the subway or bus to work, you can easily wrap up one of these meals to consume as you head to the job site. They are also very quick to make, so you can literally make your meal and head out the door. Sleeping in is no longer a reason to miss breakfast because you have some great options at your disposal.

Quick and Easy Sour Pancakes

Even the novice chef can create a tasty breakfast in just a few minutes with this recipe. This great recipe can even be included in most healthy diets.

Ingredients:

1-1/2 cups of milk
2 cups of all-purpose flour
1/4 cup of white vinegar
2 teaspoons of baking powder
1 teaspoon of baking soda
1/4 cup of white sugar
2 eggs
1 teaspoon of salt
1/4 cup of melted butter

Directions:

Mix the milk with the vinegar in a large bowl and put them aside for five minutes to create a sour taste.

While you wait, mix the sugar, baking soda, baking powder, flour and salt in a large bowl. Whisk the melted butter and the eggs into the sour milk and combine it with the sugar and flour mixture. Mix them until there are no more lumps.

Heat a large frying pan on medium heat and add cooking spray. Measure ¼ cup servings of the mixture and add them to the frying pan. Cook each pancake until bubbles appear at the surface and then flip. Cook the other side until browned.

Apple Bread Pudding

This wonderful bread pudding with a flavorful center can be enjoyed over and over again. It is even a great part of a healthy food diet.

Ingredients:

1/2 cup of apple butter
1/4 cup of raisins
3 croissants

Custard:

4 eggs
3/4 cups of sugar
1 ½ cups of 2% milk
A pinch of salt
1 teaspoon of vanilla extract

Strudel:

1/4 cup of all-purpose flour
A pinch of salt
1 tablespoon of refrigerated butter
1/4 cup of packed brown sugar

Directions:

Submerge raisins in bowling water for five minutes. Drain the water and mix the raisins with the apple butter. Split each croissant and spread the raisin and butter mixture over the bottom, then put the tops back on. Cut each croissant into thirds and place on a greased baking dish.

Custard:

Mix the eggs, sugar, milk, salt and vanilla together and pour all over the croissants. Let the croissants stand for 10 minutes to allow the custard to soak into the bread.

Strudel:

Mix the brown sugar, all-purpose flour, and salt together. Add butter slowly until the mixture looks like bread crumbs. Lightly sprinkle the mixture over the top of the croissants.

Preheat the oven to 350F and bake, uncovered, for 50 minutes.

Texas-Style French Toast

Everything is bigger in Texas, including this French toast. The key is in the apple butter and cinnamon topping for the finished product.

Ingredients:

6 slices of Texas toast
2/3 cup of milk
2 eggs
1 teaspoon of vanilla extract
2 tablespoons of almonds or hazelnuts, crushed
2 tablespoons of apple juice
Pinch of ground cinnamon
2 tablespoons of apple butter

Directions:

Mix eggs, apple juice, vanilla and milk in a bowl. Dip bread in the mixture, cover and refrigerate for at least two hours.

Place bread on a baking dish and bake, uncovered, for 30 minutes at 350F. Sprinkle hazelnuts or almonds on the warm bread. Mix the cinnamon into the apple butter and serve as a topping for the toast.

Home-style Egg Casserole

The only thing better than scrambled eggs in the morning is turning them into a great casserole that includes many food groups.

Ingredients:

1/2 cup of fresh mushrooms, sliced
5 pieces of bacon, chopped
1/4 cup of green onions, sliced
2 tablespoons of all-purpose flour
A pinch of salt
2 tablespoons of butter or margarine
A pinch of ground black pepper
3/4 cup of cheddar cheese
1 cup of skimmed milk

Scrambled Eggs:

4 large eggs
1/4 teaspoon of ground black pepper
1/4 cup of skimmed milk
A pinch of salt
1 tablespoons of parsley
2 English muffins, buttered

Directions:

Cook bacon in a frying pan until it reaches the desired level of crispiness. Set aside, while preserving 1 tablespoon of bacon fat. Cook green onions and mushrooms in the bacon fat and set aside.

Melt butter in a saucepan and slowly add flour, pepper and salt. Stir until smooth and bring the mixture to a boil. Once he mixture boils, slowly add the cheese and milk. Stir until the mixture thickens and then add crumbled bacon, mushrooms and onions. Remove from the heat and set aside.

Eggs:
Mix the eggs, milk, salt and pepper and add to a preheated frying pan. Cook over low-medium heat until the eggs set, stirring along the way.

Slice English muffins down the middle and then cut them in half. Cover the English muffins with half of the cheese sauce and then place the eggs on top. Pour the remaining cheese sauce over the eggs and then sprinkle with parsley.

Preheat the oven to 325F and cook the casserole, uncovered, for 25 minutes.

Great Start Peach Oatmeal

Starting off your day the right way often means getting some carbohydrates into your body. Oatmeal is full of energy that will keep you going until your next meal.

Ingredients:

3 cups of instant oats
6 cups of milk
1 can of diced peaches
1/2 teaspoon of sea salt
1/4 cups of Amaretto creamer
1/2 cup of white sugar

Directions:

Bring milk and salt to boil in a saucepan. Slowly add the oats and let cook for two minutes or until they have thickened. Remove the oats from the heat and stir in peaches, creamer and sugar. Serve immediately.

Southwest Breakfast Burrito

Making a breakfast burrito is an easy way to get a complete breakfast without having to eat everything individually. They are perfect for taking on the road, making it much easier to get to work on time without skipping breakfast.

Ingredients:

5 large eggs
2 radishes, sliced
2 teaspoons of lemon juice
1/2 red onion, sliced
1 avocado, chopped
Pinch of salt
1 tablespoon of butter or margarine
3 cloves of garlic, chopped
Pinch of ground black pepper
2 pork sausages, chopped
4 medium-sized tortillas
1 jalapeno pepper, sliced
1 can of pinto beans
1/4 cup green onions, sliced

Directions:

Mix radishes, red onion, lemon juice and avocado

together in a bowl. Add salt and pepper once everything has been mixed. Set aside.

Melt the butter in a skillet over medium heat and add garlic and sausage. Cook until the sausage has browned and then add beaten eggs. Stir until the eggs are scrambled to your desired consistency. Remove the skillet from the stove.

Heat the tortillas according to the direction on the package. Divide the pinto beans amongst the tortillas by spreading a thin layer of beans over the surface. Leave a 1/4 inch border. Place the scrambled eggs on top of the beans. Top with radishes and jalapeno pepper. Roll up each tortilla like a burrito and cover the finished product with a pinch of green onion.

Chapter 3: Comfort Food Lunches

There is nothing more comforting than sitting down for a nice lunch that you have prepared yourself. Rather than heading out to the local fast food joint for a quick lunch, take a look at these comfort food recipes to see what you can find. For the most part, these lunches are easy to make, so you will not spend your whole day making them.

As a bonus, many of these comfort food lunches are easy to preserve, as you can freeze them for the summer and heat them up again in the winter. Stock your freezer full of these lunches, as it gives you access to great and quick meals whenever you need them.

Finally, comfort food diet recipes are full of healthy ingredients. Any food diet that includes great tasting food is a bonus for all who partake.

As was mentioned before, many of the recipes in this book are meant for larger groups, but some of these lunches are an exception. There are recipes that are meant for one person to consume, so you can make yourself a quick lunch without even having to adjust the recipe.

Beef Barley Soup

Soup is always a great thing to have for lunch, as it is light, yet nutritious. Make a large batch of this soup and you will have it around for days afterwards. It is also very easy to freeze, so you can have it for lunch months later.

Ingredients:

1 cup of barley
5 cups of beef broth
1 large onion
4 stalks of celery
1 17-ounce steak or leftover roast beef
4 medium-sized carrots
2 cups of water
1/2 cup of puréed tomatoes
5 cloves of garlic, minced
A pinch of ground black pepper
1/2 teaspoon of salt
1 bay leaf

Directions:

Heat a large frying pan over medium heat. Coat with cooking spray and add the carrots, onion, and celery. Cook for five minutes, stirring frequently.

As the vegetables cook, cut the steak into one-inch cubes and brown the outsides.

Add garlic to the vegetables and cook for one minute. Stir in the beef, barley, broth, bay leaf, water, tomatoes, salt and pepper and bring the mixture to a boil. Once you achieve a boil, cover and simmer the soup for 40 minutes. Remove the bay leaf before serving.

French Onion Soup

What was once reserved for restaurants is now a very easy dish to make at home. The key is to bake the cheese on top of the soup once it has finished cooking.

Ingredients:

2 cups of red onion, thinly sliced
2 cups of sweet onion, thinly sliced
4 cups of beef broth
1 teaspoon of olive oil
1/4 teaspoon of ground black pepper
1/4 teaspoon of sugar
A pinch of salt
1/4 teaspoon of thyme
2 tablespoons of dry white wine
4 slices of French bread, cut into cubes
4 slices of Swiss cheese

Directions:

Heat the olive oil in a frying pan over medium-high heat and add the onions. Cook the onions until tender and then mix in the sugar, pepper and salt. Reduce the heat to medium and cook the mixture for an additional 20 minutes, stirring throughout. Increase the heat to medium-high again and sauté until the onions are a golden brown color.

Add the wine and cook for one minute.

Add the thyme and broth and bring the mixture to a boil. Cover the pan, reduce the heat and simmer the soup for two hours.

Set your oven to broil and place the bread on a baking sheet. Broil the bread for one minute on each side.

Ladle one cup of soup into an oven proof bowl and cover with cheese. Place in the oven on broil setting until the cheese is browned.

Reuben Sandwich with Turkey

This twist on the Reuben makes it easier to make, as you are more likely to have the right ingredients at the house.

Ingredients:

4 slices of rye bread
4 ounces of turkey breast
4 slices of Swiss cheese
2 tablespoons of Thousand Island dressing
1/4 cup of sauerkraut

Directions:

Spread 1/2 tablespoon of Thousand Island dressing and one slice of cheese on each slice of bread. Top each slice of cheese with 1 tablespoon of sauerkraut. Add two ounces of turkey to each sandwich and close the sandwiches.

Heat a skillet over medium heat and add the sandwiches to the pan. Press a heavy object onto the sandwich to flatten it as it cooks. Cook the sandwich for two minutes on each side or until the cheese melts.

Tuna and White Bean Salad

Beans salads go hand in hand with summer, as they provide great flavor without having to cook anything. Adding tuna turns this salad into a complete meal.

Ingredients:

1 can of white tuna
1/2 tablespoon of capers
1/2 tablespoon of parsley, chopped
10 asparagus spears
1 tablespoon of white wine vinegar
1 tablespoon of olive oil
1/2 tablespoon butter or margarine, melted
1 tablespoon of lemon juice
A pinch of salt
1/2 cup of cherry tomatoes, cubed
A pinch of ground black pepper
1 head of butter lettuce, torn
1 can of white beans

Directions:

Cover the asparagus and steam it for three minutes. Drain and rinse it in cold water to cool.

In a bowl, mix the capers, parsley, vinegar, lemon juice, olive oil, butter, salt and pepper. Add cherry tomatoes, white beans, lettuce and flaked tuna to the bowl and toss.

Spicy Chili

There is nothing like a good bowl of chili, especially when that chili is home-made. You can also add other ingredients as you see fit, as chili is a very easy dish to personalize.

Ingredients:

1 pound of ground turkey
1/2 cup of red onion, chopped
1 clove of garlic, minced
1 teaspoon of chili powder
1 poblano pepper, chopped
1/2 cup of tomato paste
1/2 teaspoon of ground cumin
A pinch of salt
1 teaspoon of dried oregano
A pinch of black pepper
2 medium tomatoes, diced
1/4 cup of cilantro
1 can of chicken broth
1 can of mixed beans, drained
3 wedges of lime

Directions:

Heat onion, poblano pepper, garlic and turkey in a large saucepan on medium. Keep on heat until the turkey is completely cooked. Combine oregano, tomato paste, salt, chili powder, pepper, beans, tomatoes, cumin, and chicken broth and bring the ingredients to a rapid boil. Reduce to a low heat and simmer for 10 minutes. Once cooked, add cilantro and serve with the wedges of lime.

Original Sloppy Joes

On those days where you have taken some ground beef out of the freezer, but do not know what to make, sloppy Joes are a definite possibility. Most of the ingredients are likely in your home already, making this an easy choice.

Ingredients:

1 1/2 pounds of ground beef
8 large cremini mushrooms, sliced
5 cloves of garlic, minced
2 tablespoons of olive oil
1/2 teaspoon salt
2 large onions, chopped
1 can of tomato paste
4 tablespoons of red wine vinegar
4 tablespoons of Worcestershire sauce
2 tablespoons of oregano, minced
2 tablespoons of honey
1 tablespoon of ground black pepper
1 teaspoon of hot sauce
8 hamburger buns or rolls, toasted

Directions:

Heat olive oil in a skillet over medium high heat and add the ground beef. Cook the beef until browned.

As the beef cooks, place mushrooms in a food processor and grind them until finely chopped. Add the mushrooms, onion, and garlic to the beef and cook until the onions are tender. Add the tomato paste, oregano, red wine vinegar, Worcestershire sauce, honey and salt to the pan and stir. Cook until the mushrooms are tender and the liquid starts to evaporate. Add pepper and hot sauce and remove from heat.

Toast each bun and top with one cup of sloppy Joe mix.

Classic Grilled Cheese Sandwich

We all love grilled cheese sandwiches because they are easy to make a wholesome. This recipe adds a little bit extra to the sandwich, making it a sure keeper.

Ingredients:
1 small clove of garlic, minced
1/2 cup of cheddar cheese, shredded
1/2 cup of red onion, sliced
1 cup of spinach
4 slices of bacon, cooked
4 slices of brown bread
2 slices of tomato

Directions:

Heat a large skillet and coat with cooking spray. Add the onion and garlic and cook until both are golden brown.

Sprinkle the shredded cheese over two slices of bread. Top each slice of bread with 1/2 cup of spinach, one tomato slice and two tablespoons of the cooked onions and garlic. Add two slices of bacon to each sandwich and top with the remaining slices of bread.

Place the sandwich in the still heated skillet and cook

until the bread is toasted and the cheese is melted.

Chicken Salad Sandwiches

Ingredients:

1 cup of skinless chicken breast, chopped
1/2 tablespoon of tarragon, chopped
1 1/2 tablespoons of Greek yogurt
1/2 tablespoon of lemon juice
1 1/2 tablespoons of mayonnaise
A pinch of salt
2 lettuce leaves
1/8 cup of sweet onion, minced
1/2 cup of arugula
4 slices of rye bread

Directions:

Mix tarragon, mayonnaise, yogurt, lemon juice, and salt in a bowl. Add chicken and onion and continue to mix. Top two pieces of bread with a lettuce leaf and add 1/2 cup of chicken mixture. Add 1/4 cup of arugula to each sandwich and top with the leftover bread.

All American Macaroni and Cheese

Macaroni might be Italian in origin, but it has a great history in North America and has become part of the cuisine. Home-made mac and cheese is much better than anything you can find in a box.

Ingredients:

4 cups of whole-wheat pasta
6 tablespoons of breadcrumbs
1/2 teaspoon of paprika
2 packages of frozen spinach, thawed
2 teaspoons of olive oil
3 1/2 cups of milk
4 cups of shredded cheddar cheese
6 tablespoons of all-purpose flour
2 cups of cottage cheese
1/2 teaspoon of salt
1/4 teaspoon of ground nutmeg
A pinch of ground pepper

Directions:

Bring a large pot of water to a boil and preheat the oven to 450F. Prepare a baking dish with cooking spray.

In a small bowl, combine oil, paprika and breadcrumbs. Strain spinach to eliminate any extra water.

Add three cups of the milk to a saucepan and heat over medium-high heat until it begins to steam. Add the remaining 1/2 cup of milk to the flour and mix until it is smooth. Add the flour and milk mixture to the hot milk, stirring continuously. Keep on heat until the sauce thickens. Remove from the heat and add cheese. Stir until the cheese has completely melted. Add nutmeg, salt, pepper and cottage cheese to the mixture.

Add pasta to the boiling water and cook until it is not quite tender, as it will keep cooking during the next portion of the process. Strain the pasta and add to the cheese sauce. Add half of the pasta mixture to the baking dish and put spinach on top. Add the rest of the pasta and top with the breadcrumbs.

Bake the pasta for 30 minutes or until the top is golden brown.

Chicken Noodle Soup for a Cold Day

As you sit and watch the snow fall in your neighborhood, there is nothing better than having a warm cup of soup in your hands. It only takes a few minutes to make a great cup of soup from scratch, which is perfect when you just want to relax.

Ingredients:

2 1/2 cups of whole-wheat noodles
8 cups of chicken broth
3/4 pound of cooked chicken breast, shredded
1 medium-sized stalk of celery, diced
2 medium-sized carrots, diced
4 cloves of garlic, minced
2 tablespoons of ginger, minced
1/2 tablespoon of lemon juice
2 tablespoons of dill, chopped

Directions:

Boil the broth in a saucepan over high heat. Reduce heat and add celery, ginger, carrots and garlic. Cook for 20 minutes over medium heat, uncovered.

Add the chicken and noodles and simmer for an

additional 10 minutes, or until the noodles are completely tender. Add dill and lemon juice before serving.

Chapter 4: Comfort Food Dinners

When you think of comfort food recipes, perhaps the main meal that you envision is dinner. This is because dinner is when families get together to talk about the day that was and to unwind before they head to bed. Comfort food is the food that we all grew up on, as we would sit down with our families and enjoy the meal.

On special occasions, we would have comfort food meals and be joined by extended family and friends. Aunts, uncles, cousins and grandparents would come to town and help us enjoy a wonderful dinner that mom had spent all day cooking.

In the end, it is more about the socialization than the food, but that does not mean that the food is not important. The food is what binds these memories together and, through the power of taste, we can rekindle these memories by making these wonderful meals at home.

Having the ability to make these wonderful meals on any day of the week allows you to recreate these special feelings for your family. These recipes are truly timeless and, thanks to the power of the internet, you can have them at your fingertips at all times.

Classic Roasted Turkey

Whether it is Thanksgiving, Christmas or just a regular Sunday in the Spring, there are plenty of reasons to cook a turkey. Rather than doing too much with the bird, use a simple recipe and let the flavor of the meat do most of the work.

Ingredients:

1 10-pound whole turkey
4 cups of turkey stock
A pinch of salt
A pinch of pepper
1/3 cup of butter, softened
1/2 teaspoon of rosemary, crushed
6 cups of stuffing

Directions:

Move oven rack to the lowest possible position and preheat the oven to 325F. Clean the turkey by removing giblets and neck and rinsing with warm water.

Place the turkey, with the breast side facing upwards, in a large roasting pan with a rack. Fill the inside of the turkey with stuffing.

Mix salt, pepper and rosemary into the butter and rub the outside of the turkey with the mixture. Pour 1 1/2 cups of turkey stock into the bottom of the pan.

Cover the roasting pan with aluminum foil and place the turkey in the oven. Baste the turkey every 30 minutes or whenever it looks dry. Add additional turkey stock to the bottom of the roasting pan when it begins to evaporate.

After 2 3/4 hours, remove the aluminum foil and cook for an additional 30 minutes for until the turkey reaches an internal temperature of 180F. Let rest for 20 minutes before carving.

Chicken Pot Pie

In today's society, it is more common to see frozen chicken pot pies from the grocery store end up on people's plates than pies made from scratch. Follow this recipe and you will wonder why you ever bought a frozen one in the first place.

Ingredients:

3 1/3 cups of chicken broth
2 pounds of skinless, chicken breasts, cubed
2 cups of peas, frozen
1 cup of celery, diced
2 cups of carrots, sliced
1/2 cup of onion, diced
1/2 cup of all-purpose white flour
1/2 cup of butter or margarine
2/3 teaspoon of salt
1/2 teaspoon of ground black pepper
1 cup of milk
1/2 teaspoon of celery seed
4 pie crusts, unbaked

Directions:

Heat oven to 425F.

Mix chicken, peas, celery and carrots in a saucepan. Add water and boil for 20 minutes. Drain and set aside for later.

Add butter and onions to a frying pan and cook over medium heat until onions are soft. Mix in flour, pepper, salt, and celery seeds. Slowly add milk and chicken broth, stirring continuously. Simmer on low-medium heat setting until it begins to thicken. Set aside
Place chicken and other ingredients at the bottom of a pie crust. Pour the milk mixture over the chicken and cover with the top of the crust. Seal the edges of the crust and remove excess dough from the sides. Make small slits in the top of the crust to prevent it from breaking while it cooks.

Bake for 30 minutes or until the top pie shell is golden brown and the inner filling begins to bubble. Allow the pie to cool for 10 minutes before serving.

Scalloped Potatoes

No matter what type of dish you are making, you will need something to accentuate it. This recipe goes great with almost every other comfort food recipe that you will find.

Ingredients:

6 large, peeled potatoes, sliced
4 tablespoons of butter or margarine
1 cup of onion, chopped
2 cups of chicken broth
1/3 cup of all-purpose flour
3 tablespoons of mayonnaise
1 teaspoon of salt
1/3 teaspoon of parsley, dried
2 1/2 garlic cloves, minced
A pinch of ground black pepper
1/2 cup of chives, chopped
1/3 teaspoon of poultry seasoning

Directions:

Preheat the oven to 325F and grease a large baking dish. Place sliced potatoes on the bottom of the dish and sprinkle onions on top.

Melt butter over medium heat and slowly add flour. Stir until the flour is completely smooth and slowly add broth, salt, parsley, poultry seasoning, pepper and mayonnaise. Cook until the mixtures thickens and begins to bubble.

Pour mixture over the potatoes and onions. Cover the dish with aluminum foil and place in the oven for about 2 hours, or whenever the potatoes are fully cooked. Remove foil for the final 15 minutes of cooking to allow them to brown. Sprinkle with chives before you serve.

Potato Salad

Dinners in the summer are not complete without potato salad, especially if you are eating outside. Finish up your barbeque by using this great variation of this classic dish.

Ingredients:

4 pounds of potatoes, chopped
1/2 cup of olive oil
2 tablespoons of Dijon mustard
4 tablespoons of balsamic vinegar
1 teaspoon of salt
1/2 teaspoon of freshly ground black pepper
4 tablespoons of basil, chopped
1 1/2 cups of blue cheese, crumbled
1 cup of onion, chopped
4 tablespoons of chives, chopped

Directions:

Bring potatoes to a boil in lightly salted water. Reduce heat and simmer for 15 minutes or until the potatoes are tender. Drain the water and set aside.

Combine olive oil, vinegar, salt, pepper and basil in a bowel. Add potatoes and onion, tossing to coat in the mixture. Let the potatoes cool for an additional 30 minutes.

Add blue cheese and chives to the other ingredients and stir well.

Easy Pork (or lamb) Chops

Pork chops are in everyone's recipe book, but this simple recipe allows you to make a variation of your favorite dish.

Ingredients:

6 pork loin chops
1 cup of canned apricots
2 1/2 tablespoons of Dijon mustard
3/4 cup of Italian salad dressing

Directions:

Mix apricots, Italian dressing and mustard in a bowl and pour into a freezer bag. Add the pork chops to the mixture and place in refrigerator for at least eight hours, turning halfway through the marinating process.

Preheat a propane grill on medium heat. Remove pork chops from the bag and discard the marinade. Place marinated pork chops on the grill and cook for five minutes on each side or until the meat reaches an internal temperature of 145F. Let the meat stand for five to seven minutes before serving.

Southern-Style Pulled Pork

Pulled pork is now popular all over the country, but it got its start in the south. The chipotle pepper gives the sandwich a little more bite, but can be substitute for those who avoid spicy foods.

Ingredients:

1 4 pound pork (or lamb) loin roast
1/2 cup of onion, chopped
4 cloves of garlic, minced
2 cups of barbecue sauce
1/2 teaspoon of salt
1/4 teaspoon of pepper
1 teaspoon of cumin, ground
2 chipotle peppers, chopped
1 block of cheddar cheese, sliced
2 tomatoes, sliced
1 1/2 cups of mayonnaise
1 loaf of sourdough bread

Directions:

Place the roast in a slow cooker. Mix the onion, garlic, cumin, salt, pepper and barbecue sauce together and pour over the pork. Cook on low heat for at least seven hours or until the meat is completely tender. Remove the meat from the slow cooker and allow it to cool for 15 minutes. Shred the roast with two forks and return the meat to the slow cooker. Reheat the meat.

Cut bread into your desired number of slices and desired thickness. Broil bread for two minutes on each side or until it is a golden brown color.

Mix chipotle pepper with mayonnaise and spread on the bread. Place pork mixture on the bread and top with cheese and tomatoes. Cover with another piece of bread to finish the sandwich.

Slow Cooker Ribs

Good ribs take time to make properly, which is where a slow cooker comes into play. Take your time and your ribs will be fall-off-the-bone delicious.

Ingredients:

5 pounds of pork (or lamb) back ribs
2 teaspoons of ground black pepper
3 cups of barbecue sauce
1 large clove of garlic, minced
2 tablespoons of Dijon mustard
1 can of cherries

Directions:

Using a knife, divide the ribs into easy to eat sizes. Sprinkle pepper on outside of ribs and move the ribs to the slow cooker. Mix the barbeque sauce, cherries, mustard and garlic together and place on top of the ribs. Set the cooker on low for eight hours. When completed, the meat should fall off the bone.

All-American Diner Cheeseburger

Rather than heading down to the diner to buy a cheeseburger, try making one on your own. It is always better to make these items at home, as you have full control over the quality of the ingredients.

Ingredients:

2 pounds of ground beef
4 tablespoons of ketchup
1 large garlic clove, minced
1 medium onion, diced
2 teaspoon of Worcestershire sauce
2 teaspoon of white sugar
1/2 teaspoon of apple cider vinegar
2 teaspoon of steak sauce
1 package of bacon, cooked
8 slices of cheddar cheese
8 hamburger buns, toasted

Directions:

Mix the onion, ketchup, garlic, sugar, Worcestershire sauce, steak sauce and apple cider vinegar in a large bowl. Add the ground beef to the mixture and continue to stir until the beef is thoroughly coated. Shape the ground beef into large patties.

Preheat the grill on medium and cook hamburgers for five to seven minutes on each side or until the juices run clear. Top the burger with cheese and grill for an additional minute or until the cheese is completely melted. Add bacon to the top of the burger and place on a toasted bun. Add additional toppings of your choosing.

Grandma’s Beef Stew

Grandmas seem to have a way with stews, as there is always something different about eating at her house. With this recipe, you can take grandma's stew any time you need a hearty meal.

Ingredients:

2 1/2 pounds of stewing beef, cubed
1 1/2 tablespoon of olive oil
2/3 teaspoon of seasoning salt
2/3 teaspoon ground black pepper
1 cup of all-purpose flour
3 tablespoons of Worcestershire sauce
1 large onion, sliced
1 1/2 tablespoons of lemon juice
1 1/2 teaspoon of white sugar
2 large cloves of garlic, minced
2/3 teaspoon of paprika
2/3 teaspoon of salt
1/4 teaspoon of allspice, ground
8 medium-sized carrots, peeled and sliced
6 medium-sized potatoes, peeled and cubed
1 bay leaf, whole
2 cups of water

Directions:

Mix 3/4 cup of flour, 1/4 teaspoon of black pepper and seasoning salt in a freezer bag. Add cubed stewing beef a few pieces at a time and coat in flour.

Heat olive oil in a frying pan over medium-high heat and add coated beef a few pieces at a time. Brown the meat and set aside.

Add water to the frying pan and scrape leftover brown bits that are stuck on the pan. Add Worcestershire sauce, onion, lemon juice, sugar, garlic, allspice, bay leaf, salt, remaining pepper and paprika to the pan while stirring. Return the browned stew beef to the pan and bring to a boil. Reduce heat, cover and simmer for one hour.

Add potatoes and carrots to the stew and stir well. Increase heat until the mixture boils again then reduce heat to medium-low, cover and simmer for 30 minutes.

Once everything has been cooked, add remaining flour to water and stir until it is smooth. Add the mixture to the stew, stirring constantly. Bring to a boil and let thicken for two minutes. Remove bay leaf and service.

Meat Loaf

Meat loaf comes in a variety of forms, as everyone seems to have their own take on this classic comfort food recipe. Adding the right balance of ingredients is important because it ensures that the flavor of the meat is accented, rather than overshadowed.

Ingredients:

1 pound of ground pork (or lamb)
1 pound of ground beef
1 medium-sized onion, finely chopped
1 tablespoon of olive oil
1 medium-sized green pepper, finely chopped
2 cloves of garlic, minced
3/4 cup of milk
1 large egg, beaten
4 slices bread, ground
1/3 cup of maple syrup
1 teaspoon of rosemary, crushed
1/2 cup of cheddar cheese, grated
1 teaspoon of salt
1 cup of ketchup
1 teaspoon of ground black pepper
1 tablespoon of apple cider vinegar

Directions:

Cook green pepper and onion in a frying pan until tender. Add garlic and cook for one additional minute. Remove from heat and set aside to cool.

In a mixing bowl, combine eggs, bread, milk, cheese, salt, pepper and rosemary. Add green pepper and onion to the bowl. Add ground beef and pork to the mixture and mix extremely well.

Place meatloaf in a loaf pan and compress. Mix ketchup, maple syrup and vinegar together and spread over the top of the meatloaf.

Preheat the oven to 350F and bake, uncovered, for 60 minutes or until the meat is completely cooked. Let cool for 10 minutes before serving.

Down South Beef Brisket

The south loves its brisket and knows how to do it right. This recipe allows you to bring southern-style cooking into your home, no matter where in the country you live.

Ingredients:

1 4-pound beef brisket
2 stalks of celery, sliced
2 large, peeled potatoes, sliced
1 medium onion, sliced
1 tablespoon olive oil
1 can of lager-style beer
2 cloves of garlic, minced
2/3 teaspoon of beef bouillon
1/2 cup of tomato paste
1 cup of tomatoes, stewed
1/3 cup of red wine vinegar
4 tablespoons of Dijon mustard
4 tablespoons of brown sugar
4 tablespoons of soy sauce
2/3 teaspoons of paprika
2 1/2 tablespoons of maple syrup
1/3 teaspoon of salt
1 bay leaf

1/4 teaspoon of ground black pepper

Directions:

Place celery and potatoes in a slow cooker. Cut the brisket in half and brown each side in a frying pan using the olive oil. Place the browned brisket in the slow cooker. Cook the onions in the same frying pan until tender. Add the garlic to the pan and cook for one additional minute. Add the onions and the garlic to the slow cooker.

Stir beer and beef bouillon together in the frying pan and then pour over the meat in the slow cooker.

Put lid on the cooker and cook, on low, for 10 hours or until meat is completely tender. Remove bay leaf and discard. Slice the meat against the grain and serve.

Old Fashioned Ham Steak

Ham steaks are not as popular as they once were, but that does not make them any less delicious. Try this recipe on the grill or on a skillet during the winter.

Ingredients:

1 2-pound ham steak
1 teaspoon of fresh lemon juice
2 teaspoons of mustard
1/3 cup of canned apricots or plums
A pinch of cinnamon, ground

Directions:

Mix fruit, mustard, cinnamon and lemon juice together in a sauce pan. Heat on low for three minutes and set aside.

Score the ham and brush with the glaze. Place on grill preheated to medium heat and cook for 10 minutes on each side, adding more glaze over the final three minutes.

Honey Baked Ham

Livening up a baked ham is a great way to keep the family interested. Serve this meal with some mashed potatoes and you have a sure winner on your hands.

Ingredients:

1 whole ham, precooked
1/2 cup of honey
1 can of pineapple, sliced
1 teaspoon of mustard, ground
2 teaspoons of apple cider vinegar
1 clove, ground
6 Maraschino cherries

Directions:

Drain the pineapple, but retain the juice. Set aside.

Preheat oven for 350F and bake ham, uncovered, for 30 minutes.

Combine honey, mustard, vinegar, cloves and two tablespoons of pineapple juice in a bowl. Score the skin of the ham. Place pineapple slices and cherries on top of the ham and cover with glaze. Bake for an additional 45 minutes and serve.

Spaghetti and Meatballs

This classic Italian meal has made its way into homes all over the world because it is easy to make and provides great flavor.

Ingredients:

3 cans of pureed tomatoes, (approximately 30 ounces)
2 cloves of garlic, minced
1 medium onion, chopped
2 tablespoons of extra virgin olive oil
2 cups of water
1 can of tomato paste
1/3 cup of Parmesan cheese, grated
2 teaspoons of salt
2 teaspoons of oregano, dried
2 teaspoons of white sugar

Meatballs:

1/2 pound of ground pork (or lamb)
3/4 pound of ground beef
4 large eggs, lightly beaten
3/4 cup breadcrumbs
1 clove of garlic, minced
3/4 teaspoon oregano, dried

2 tablespoons Parmesan cheese, grated
1 package of spaghetti or other pasta, cooked

Directions:

In a frying pan, cook onion and garlic in oil over medium heat until cooked. Add tomatoes, tomato paste, water, cheese, oregano salt and sugar to the pan and simmer, uncovered, for 90 minutes.

Mix pork, beef and breadcrumbs together and set aside. Mix eggs, cheese, oregano and garlic together and add to meat. Mix well.

Shape meat mixture into balls and brown the outside in a frying pan. Add the meatballs to the sauce and simmer for an additional 90 minutes. Serve the meatballs and the sauce on top of the spaghetti.

Sunday Pot Roast

Memories of special Sunday dinners are present in everyone's head, as we have all had those special moments with family. The good news is that you can make a pot roast very quickly, so you do not have to spend the day inside cooking it if you wish to have your own special Sunday get together.

Ingredients:

1 4-pound beef chuck roast
8 tablespoons of butter or margarine
8 tablespoons of all-purpose flour
6 carrots, peeled and chopped
4 cups of water
1 large onion, chopped
1 celery stalk, chopped
3 teaspoons of beef bouillon
1 tablespoon of salt
2/3 teaspoon of ground black pepper

Directions:

Sprinkle 1-1/2 teaspoons of flour onto the roast and heat a large frying pan with 4 tablespoons of butter. Brown all sides of the beef over medium heat. Add water, onion, celery, pepper, salt and bouillon to the frying pan and cover. Simmer for one hour.. Add the water, bouillon, onion, celery, salt and pepper; bring to a boil. Reduce heat, cover and simmer for one hour.

Add carrots to the pan and cook for an additional 60 minutes or until the cook is completely cooked. Remove the carrots and meat from the pan and set aside. Strain meat juices and set aside.

Add the remaining butter to the frying pan and slowly add flour. Cook the mixture until it bubbles. Add two cups of the meat juices to the butter and flour mixture and stir until it is smooth. Cook until it is thickened to desired level.

Stick to Your Ribs Shepherd's Pie

Shepherd's pie is a classic dish that goes back to the days of shepherds tending to their sheep. There is no doubt that this recipe is better than anything that they had out in the fields.

Ingredients:

1 pound of ground beef, pork or lamb
2/3 cup of beef broth
10 medium potatoes, cubed
1/3 cup of warm skimmed milk
2 cloves of garlic, minced
2 tablespoons of olive oil
1 medium onion
2 teaspoons of tomato paste
1 cup of mushrooms, chopped
1 teaspoon of horseradish, grated
1 teaspoon of salt
1/3 teaspoon of ground black pepper
1 teaspoon of mustard, ground
1/3 cup of red pepper, chopped
1/3 cup of green pepper, chopped
1 cup cheddar cheese, shredded

Directions:

Heat olive oil in a skillet and add ground beef, onion and garlic. Cook until browned. Add mushrooms and cook for an additional three minutes or until the mushrooms are tender.

Put tomato paste in a bowl and slowly add broth from the skillet. Mix until smooth and then add horseradish, mustard, salt and pepper. Add tomato paste mixture to the beef and stir. Place in a baking pan.

Cook peppers in the skillet until they are tender and place on top of the meat.

Boil the potatoes until they are tender and drain. Mix with milk and cheese and place over top of peppers.

Bake, uncovered, at 425F for 15 minutes and then reduce heat to 350F before baking for an additional 20 minutes.

Simple Ham and Chicken Casserole

Casserole is a great comfort food recipe because leftovers can be used to create it. If you have some spare ingredients from the night before, give this easy recipe a try.

Ingredients:

2 cups of cooked chicken, diced
2 cups of cooked ham, cubed
2 tablespoons of butter or margarine
1 large onion, chopped
1/3 cup of red pepper, chopped
1 cup of fresh mushrooms, diced
1 cup of black olives
3/4 cup of sour cream
1/3 teaspoon of pepper
1 teaspoon of salt
1 can of cream of mushroom soup
1 package of noodles, cooked and drained
2 tablespoons of Parmesan cheese, shredded

Directions:

Heat butter in a frying pan and cook onion until tender. Mix chicken, ham, olives, pepper, mushrooms, soup, sour cream, pepper, salt and onion in a bowl. Add cooked noodles and stir well.

Pour entire mixture into a baking dish and sprinkle cheese on top. Bake, uncovered, for 45 minutes at 325F.

Fried Whole Chicken

You do not have to live in the south to appreciate fried chicken, especially when it can be cooked in a matter of minutes. Cooking it yourself allows you to avoid the heavy oils that are used by many fried chicken restaurants.

Ingredients:

1 4-pound broiler chicken, cut into pieces
2 teaspoons of salt
2 cups of all-purpose flour
1 teaspoon of ground black pepper
1 teaspoon of garlic powder
Oil or lard for frying

Directions:

Place flour, salt, garlic powder and black pepper in a freezer bag. Add the chicken to the bag one piece at a time, coating in the flour mixture.

Pour 1/2 inch of oil or lard into a large frying pan. Heat oil or lard over medium-high heat and add chicken to the pan. Cook until the chicken is browned on each time and then reduce heat. Cook for an additional 35 minutes, covered, on low-medium heat, turning every 10 minutes. Uncover the chicken and cook for an additional five minutes.

Easy Cabbage Rolls

Cabbage rolls might not be for everyone, but those who like them tend to like them a lot. This recipe uses an outstanding medley of flavors that makes it very unique.

Ingredients:

1/2 pound of ground pork
1/2 pound of ground beef
8 large cabbage leaves
2 cups of tomato juice
1 cup rice, cooked
1 medium onion, chopped
2 teaspoon of Worcestershire sauce
2 eggs
1 teaspoon of Dijon mustard
4 tablespoons of brown sugar

Directions:

Bring water to a boil in a large saucepan and cook cabbage for five minutes. Drain the water and set aside. In a large frying pan, brown the ground beef, pork and onion over medium heat. Cook until meat is no longer pink on the outside. Add rice, mustard, eggs and Worcestershire sauce to the meat and stir well.

Place 1/3 of a cup of meat mixture onto each cabbage leaf, fold the sides and roll the leaf tightly. Place each leaf in a baking dish with the seam side down.

Pour tomato juice over cabbage rolls and sprinkle brown sugar on top. Cover and bake for 50 minutes at 350F. Remove the lid from the baking pan and cook for an additional 10 minutes.

Chicken and Dumplings

When "she" comes around the mountain, you will be happy that you have this recipe. Chicken and dumplings is a classic country meal that will stick with you until the morning.

Ingredients:

1 8-pound chicken, cut into pieces
2 cups of all-purpose flour
4 teaspoons of salt
6 teaspoons of paprika
1 cup of onion
1/2 cup of butter
3 cups of chicken broth
1 cup of celery

Dumplings:

2 cups of all-purpose flour
1 teaspoon of salt
2 teaspoons of baking powder
1 cup of milk
2 eggs

Gravy:

4 tablespoons of arrowroot powder
1 cup of sour cream
2 tablespoons of parsley, minced
4 tablespoons of water

Directions:

Combine flour 3 teaspoons of paprika, and salt in a freezer bag. Add chicken and seal the bag. Toss the bag to coat.

Heat a frying pan over medium heat and add butter. Brown the chicken in the butter a few pieces at a time and set aside.

Use the same frying pan to sauté the celery and onion. Add the chicken, broth and the rest of the paprika. Cover the pan and simmer on medium-low heat for 45 minutes. Remove the chicken.

Prepare the dumplings by mixing flour, baking powder and salt in a bowl. Add eggs and milk and stir well. This will create a dough. Scoop the dough with a tablespoon and drop into the broth. Cover and continue simmering the broth for 10 minutes. Remove the dumplings.

To make the gravy, mix arrowroot powder into water and stir the mixture into the broth. Bring the gravy to a boil and cook it for two minutes. Reduce the heat to medium-low and add sour cream and parsley. Serve everything together.

Chapter 5: Comfort Food Desserts

You might not have room for dessert after one of these delicious comfort food dinners, but that you not stop you from trying them out. Comfort food desserts are just like the ones that you had growing up. Before all of the fancy dessert boutiques and high-priced bakeries existed, we ate desserts featuring seasonal ingredients. These ingredients are always on the shelves, making these desserts easy to make for even an inexperienced chef.

Classic American Banana Split

The banana split is about as American as it gets, as it is a classic dessert from years gone by. It is also one of the simplest desserts that you can possibly make, as it only takes a matter of minutes.

Ingredients:

2 scoops of chocolate ice cream
2 scoops of vanilla ice cream
2 scoops of strawberry ice cream

2 bananas, split
2 tablespoons of chocolate syrup
4 tablespoons of whipping cream
4 tablespoons of strawberries, sliced
4 tablespoons of pineapple, sliced
4 maraschino cherries
2 tablespoons of nuts, chopped

Directions:

Place bananas in a large dish and place ice cream between the slices. Top ice cream with whipping cream, strawberries, chocolate sauce and peanuts. Place cherries on top.

Simple Angel Food Cake

Angel food cake is a light and fluffy dessert that can be dressed up any way that you desire. Its versatility is what makes it such a great comfort food.

Ingredients:

5 egg whites
1/2 cup of all-purpose flour
1/2 tablespoon of powdered sugar
3/4 teaspoon of vanilla extract
3/4 teaspoon of cream of tartar
1/2 cup of white sugar
1/4 teaspoon of almond extract

Directions:

Put egg whites into a bowl and set aside for 30 minutes.

Use a sifter to mix powdered sugar and flour together.

Mix cream of tartar, vanilla extract, almond extract and salt with the egg whites using a beater on medium speed. Slowly add the white sugar, two tablespoons at a time, while beating the mixture on high. Eventually, glossy peaks will form and the sugar will be completely dissolved. Fold the flour and powdered sugar mixture into the bowl 1/4 cup at a time.

Spoon the mixture into a pan and cut through it with a knife to remove any air pockets that have formed. Preheat oven at 350F and cook for 40 minutes or until the top is lightly browned. Let cool for at least one hour and add icing to the finished product if desired.

Harvest Apple Pie

Few things bring about memories of the fall and the Thanksgiving season like a warm apple pie. This recipe is for a classic apple pie, with a few new flavors that are sure to add to the overall taste of the dish. Serve with a roasted turkey dinner to complete the Thanksgiving meal.

Ingredients:

14 tart apples, peeled and sliced
1 cup of brown sugar
1 cup of white sugar
2 teaspoons of cinnamon
1/3 cup of all-purpose flour
1/4 teaspoon of nutmeg, ground
1/2 teaspoon of ginger, ground
2 tablespoons of lemon juice
2 tablespoons of butter
2 egg whites
2 double-crust pie shells

Directions:

In a bowl, mix white sugar, brown sugar, flour, cinnamon, ginger and nutmeg. In a separate bowl, mix apples with lemon juice. Add the sugar and spices and toss to coat.

Place the bottom pie crust in a pie plate and fill with the apple mixture. Repeat with the second pie shell. Spread 1 tablespoon of butter over top of each pie and cover each pie with the top of the shell.

Use a beater to mix egg whites until they foam. Brush the egg whites over the top of the pie and sprinkle sugar on top if desired. Cover the pie with aluminum foil.

Preheat the oven to 375F and cook for 25 minutes. Remove the foil and cook for another 20 minutes or until the top of the pie is a golden brown color.

Cheesecake Pie

Traditional cheesecake takes some time to make, but a cheesecake pie can be ready to eat in a couple of hours. The key is in the crust, as it provides texture for this great dessert.

Ingredients:

2 packages of cream cheese
1-1/3 cups of graham crackers, crushed
1/3 cup of white sugar
1/2 cup of butter, melted
2 eggs, beaten
Lemon zest to taste
1-1/2 teaspoons of vanilla extract

Topping:

4 teaspoons of white sugar
1-1/4 cups of sour cream
2/3 teaspoons of vanilla

Directions:

Mix graham cracker crumbs with butter and press onto the bottom and sides of a pie plate. Cover and put in the refrigerator for at least 30 minutes.

Use beaters to mix cream cheese and sugar until smooth. Add eggs and continue to mix. Add vanilla and lemon peel and stir. Pour the mixture into the cooled crust.

Preheat the oven to 325F and bake for 25 minutes. Remove from the oven and let cool for five minutes, but do not turn oven off. Mix sour cream, vanilla and sugar together and spread over the pie. Put back in oven for an additional five minutes. Refrigerate until you are ready to serve.

Cherry Crisp

Nothing says summer like fresh cherries and by including this wonderful ingredient in with your dessert, you can make something that the entire family will enjoy. This healthy dessert can also be enjoyed as part of a nutritious breakfast.

Ingredients:

Pastry:

2 cups of all-purpose flour
1 cup of brown sugar
1/2 teaspoons of salt
1 cup of butter, cubed

Filling:

8 cups of red cherries, pitted
2 cups of sugar
2 cups of cherry juice
1/2 cup of arrowroot powder

Topping:

3 cups of instant oats

1/2 cup of all-purpose flour
1 cup of brown sugar
1/2 cup of butter, melted

Directions:

Mix sugar, flour and salt in a bowl and cut in butter. Press into a baking pan and cook on 350F for 15-20 minutes.

Make filling by mixing sugar and arrowroot powder in a saucepan and stirring in cherry juice. Cook on medium heat until it thickens, stirring often. Add cherries and pour over the crust.

Mix oats brown sugar, flour and butter together and sprinkle over the filling.

Bake at 350F for an additional 25 minutes or until the topping turns golden brown.

Chapter 6: Your Comfort Food Meal Plan

With so many comfort foods from which to choose, it can be difficult to decide on where to start. This sample meal plan gives you a great start by allowing you to fit comfort food into your already existing diet.

The basic idea is that you continue to follow your current diet, but you mix in some comfort food to keep your taste buds happy.

Day One:

Start your week with a healthy breakfast of your choice.

Have some beef barley soup and a grilled cheese sandwich for lunch.

Complete your day with a healthy dinner and a cheesecake pie for dessert.

Day Two:

Get started with a southwest breakfast burrito, as it includes all of the food groups that you need to start your day the right way.

Heat up some leftover beef barley soup to supplement your lunch.

Stick to a healthy dinner.

Day Three:

Make some peach oatmeal to give yourself the energy that you need.

Have a healthy lunch, but be sure that you save room for dinner.

Make some All-American cheeseburgers for the family to enjoy. Add scalloped potatoes or whatever else you desire to the meal. Have a banana split for dessert.

Day Four:

Quick and easy sour pancakes provide a great start to the day and will provide you with energy.

A light lunch to keep you going throughout the afternoon.

Go with the honey baked ham at night, as it is a quick meal and extremely filling.

Day Five:

Eat a breakfast of your choice, but make sure that it is filling and provides energy.

Have some chili for lunch, as it is easy to make and the leftovers can be saved for another day.

Make sure of your leftover ham from the previous night and make a chicken and ham casserole.

As you can see, you do not have to include comfort food in every meal, but having it for at least one meal per day does liven things up considerably. Many of these meals are large enough that you will surely have leftovers for the next day, which is great news because it makes that day much easier. The soups that are found in these recipes are also very adaptable, as you can throw whichever leftovers you have from the previous night in with the soup.

This is why so many people are now choosing to begin a comfort food diet, as it is an easy way to get the most from your food. This style of diet provides you with the calories that you need, while spreading them out between your meals, which provides you with a steady stream of energy during your daily endeavors.

Chapter 7: Eating with Comfort in Mind

Of course, there is more that goes into choosing a meal plan than comfort, but how much you like the food that you are eating is definitely important. These recipes have been designed with taste in mind, but that does not mean that they are unhealthy. Heart healthy alternatives like olive oil are used whenever possible. While there is fat found in many of these recipes, it is not excessive. In fact, a healthy amount of fat can be beneficial, as it provides additional energy if you do not eat enough carbohydrates.

Many of these recipes have been inspired by recipes that are found online. This should not come as a surprise because most of these foods have been popular in the United States for generations. Some of them are new takes on these items, while others are just classic American meals. The point of this book is to let people know that you do not have to eat foods that you do not enjoy just to stay healthy. There is a balance between eating what is right and eating what is delicious and that it what this book aims to provide.

Before starting on these recipes, it is a good idea to learn about what your body needs to stay healthy. Many diets that are currently on the market do not provide human beings with the bare necessities. This is why people plateau with their weight loss, as their bodies are not being given the proper fuel. Fueling your body is as much about how much you put into it as it is about what you put into it, which is something that you must remember when dieting.

Eating for Health and Pleasure

Many different fad diets exist that promise to help you lose large amounts of weight quickly, but the majority of these diets do not work long term. A balanced diet can help you to lose weight and will provide you with all of the nutrients that your body needs to stay healthy, making it the best diet for you to follow.

While many people diet because they want to lose weight, not every weight loss program provides health benefits for an individual. When you do not follow a balanced diet, you might lose some weight, but also run the risk of running into problems with your muscle development, your brain function and the maintenance of your body's tissues. Therefore, you should make sure that your diet helps you meet your nutritional needs, in addition to helping you lose weight.

When choosing the ingredients for your comfort food diet, you should follow a few simple rules. According to the National Institutes of Health, you should select low fat dairy products, lean cuts of beef, poultry, fish and pork, eat plenty of fruits and vegetables and stick with whole grains as part of your diet. All of these foods hold nutritional value and will help you to lose weight when consumed in moderation.

You must remember that portion control remains an important part of a balanced diet, since eating too much of anything will lead to weight gain. You can begin by only taking one serving of each item that you eat and if you must go for seconds, make it a vegetable product.

Your level of nutrition will increase substantially once you begin a balanced diet, as you will get everything that your body needs to function at a high level. This will increase your energy levels, which will make sure that you accomplish your goals every day. This will also decrease your chances of getting certain diseases, making it worth the effort on every level.

Getting the Most for Your Money

Whenever the economy goes through a downturn, getting the most for your money becomes all the more important. Eating out is no longer an option for many people, especially those who have been directly affected by the recent economic crash.

At the same time, most people do not have the culinary expertise to construct the fine dining experience at home. The cooks who put the menus together in fancy restaurants have years of experience and put all of their time into create that food. You do not have the luxury of spending all of your time creating a menu or experimenting with flavors until you find a new and exciting dish.

What you do have at your disposal, however, is comfort food. This food is easy to make and will not set you back the way eating out does. You can head to the grocery store, pick up a few ingredients and make a meal that everyone will enjoy for very little money. This is how you get the most out of your meals, as these comfort food recipes will fill you up at dinner, while leaving enough left over for you to eat at lunch.

You do not have to head to a fancy restaurant to get an outstanding meal because you have the ability to make that meal from the comfort of your own home. It will not be anything fancy, like what you will see at a French restaurant downtown, but it will be good, wholesome food that will be enjoyed by the entire family. That is what comfort food is all about and what it will continue to be about for generations to come.

Comfort Food - a Summary

"Comfort Food Diet: Comfort Food Recipes For Comfort Food Lovers" is an excellent collection of comfort food recipes that the whole family can enjoy. With so many cookbooks now focusing on low-fat or low-calorie diets, it is nice to find a comfort food diet cookbook that considers the enjoyment that people actually get out of the food. The comfort food diet recipes found in this book are unique takes on classic American recipes like that ones that you likely had growing up. By putting them in a collection, this book provides an easily accessible place to keep all of these great recipes of years gone by.

Another great thing about this book is that every comfort food recipe is made with items that are found in most kitchens. It is very discouraging to find a great book of recipes, only to find that many of the ingredients are obscure. If you are on a comfort foods diet, you likely want easily accessible ingredients, so you can make the recipes at any time of the day. This collection ensures that you will never run into problems making this diet comfort food.

In addition to great recipes, this book gives information on what is to be included in healthy diets. There is a great deal of misinformation out there regarding what makes up a healthy food diet. For example, many people now avoid eating carbohydrates, but all that does is create an energy deficiency, which makes it more difficult to actually burn calories. This food lovers diet will provide you with the energy that you need to get through the day, without leaving yourself feeling drained. If you are serious about starting a food diet, you should look to one that allows you to actually eat.

Overall, this collection provides everything that you could ever want out of a cookbook. It has excellent recipes and it includes information on how to make these recipes work for you as you attempt to make yourself healthier.

www.ingramcontent.com/pod-product-compliance
Ingram Content Group UK Ltd.
Pitfield, Milton Keynes, MK11 3LW, UK
UKHW020142250726
13967UKWH00002B/817

9 781633 830721